Walking in the Light

A Pentecostal Perspective
on the Christian Life

by
James M. Beaty

Derek Press
Cleveland, Tennessee

Walking in the Light
Copyright 2004, by James M. Beaty
All rights reserved

Copies of articles
may be made for classroom use
and for other non-profit ministry uses.

Library of Congress
Catalog Card Number 2004109944
ISBN 0-87148-091-3

Set in Times New Roman and Monotype Cursiva
by the author and
Printed by Derek Press,
Cleveland, Tennessee, United States of America

To my wife
Virginia Green Beaty
My faithful companion

&

Mark, Jamie, Isaiah, & Carmen
Our beloved son and family

And now let us breath a prayer
That God will open our understanding.

Oh, our God, teach us thy word,
Let the light of the Holy Spirit shine on thy truth;
Help us to see our privileges in Christ Jesus.
As thou dost open thy word to us,
Help us to walk in the light.
Oh, make us perfect as thou art perfect.
Oh, our mighty Heavenly Father,
Let a tidal way of thy glory and love sweep over us,
Till the whole is lost in God:
For Jesus' sake, Amen!

Carl Padgett

Foreword

In *Walking in the Light* Dr. James M. Beaty shares personal insights with the reader from his life-long experiences as a minister, theologian, missionary and teacher. From some of his own sermons, articles and scholarly presentations, he defines what it means to be a child of God and to "walk in the light." This is a man of God who has dedicated his life to the call of God and who has personally taken the truth of the Gospel message to many living in spiritual darkness.

Dr. Beaty discusses various aspects of the Christian life from a Pentecostal perspective as he powerfully shares from the word of God. He also deals with crucial elements of the Pentecostal experience giving both resource information and practical helps.

As a missionary to Haiti with his wonderful wife and partner in ministry, Virginia, he knows what it means to respond to the Great Commission and follow where God leads. He discusses the mission of the church with great commitment and conviction. He also reminds the reader that our task is either to go or to send—but that we are all involved in this calling.

James Beaty heard and answered the call of God and with the voice of experience he challenges the reader to "walk in the light." You will be blessed and your life enriched as you read these scholarly and inspiring expositions.

R. Lamar Vest
General Overseer of the Church of God
August, 2003

Acknowledgments

I hereby acknowledge and thank all those who have assisted me in my ministry and writing in whatever way. Since these articles span about fifty years, it is difficult to name all the names. But my wife is first of all. I take very seriously the fact that, in marriage, one plus one equals one. We married as she was finishing college and I was finishing seminary. But I would not have been able to do my Ph.D. if it had not been for the fact that she became the bread-winner by teaching in a high school.

Various secretaries in Haiti, in South America, in Houston and at the Theological Seminary typed on some of the earlier copies of these articles for publication in English, Spanish and French. Some of my secretaries and student workers while I was Dean of the Theological Seminary put the material on the computer. And since I have retired, I have done the editing and type-setting as it now appears.

Thanks to the *Church of God Evangel* for having previously published five of the articles; to the Spanish *El Evangélio* for having published two and the Haitian *L'Evangile* for having published one. L.W. Sisk, who wrote the article on "Entire Sanctification," has been with the Lord over fifty years. I trust that the digest of his little book will honor his name and memory.

I also thank the various authors which I have cited and duly acknowledged in the different articles. To all of these and many more I am indebted. But most of all I am indebted to Him "Whose I am and Whom I serve." To Him be the Glory forever and ever.

James M. Beaty

Preface

This is a collection of articles written over a period of many years. Some have been published and some have not. Some were published in English, some in Spanish and one in French. This was due to the nature of our ministry in different parts of Latin America: Dominican Republic, Haiti, and South America. For the last thirty-five years my ministry has been here in the United States, involved in education: Lee University, where I taught Bible and Ethics for seven years, Spanish Institute of Ministry, where I was founder and president for six years, and Church of God Theological Seminary, where I was Academic Dean for twelve years (1980-92) and taught part-time until 2001.

Since this is a collection of writings, it is clear the title of the book, "Walking in the Light." was chosen to pull together the different threads of thought in the articles. If it had been the other way around, the content, in many ways, would have been quite different. "Walking in the Light," a term often used when I joined the Church of God (1940), meant 'seeking to know and obey the will of God as understood through His Word and the light shed upon the Word by the Holy Spirit.'

These articles were written in many different situations, but mostly where adequate library facilities were not available. And most of them were written for the laity. And the rest are affected by my attempt at simplicity and clarity. When your ministry is done in several languages, you soon realize that eloquence is not the prime target. Most of what is contained in these articles was not learned in college, seminary or the university, but in ministry, with the help of the Spirit of God, as I used the tools acquired in the educational process.

The articles are organized into four parts, 'Pentecostal Experience,' 'The Christian Life,' 'Christmas, Easter and Pentecost', and 'The Mission of the Church.' I trust that both

Pentecostals and non-Pentecostals, who read this book, shall be inspired and encouraged to "walk in the light," and to seek a deeper walk with the Lord. May we come to a fuller realization of who we are as parts of the body of Christ, which he wants to use in order to carry out his mission and ministry in the world today.

Apart from the articles, there is a short digest of a booklet on "Entire Sanctification" by the Reverend Leonard W. Sisk, a Church of God minister, now deceased.

I have a debt of gratitude to many people: the teachers who taught me, "those over me in the Lord," those whom I have taught and who, in turn, taught me, as well as all those who are part of the body of Christ where I have had the privilege to minister. It is wonderful to have a family all around the world, who loves and appreciates you, even when they are unaware of your ministry in other areas of the world.

I would, especially, like to acknowledge with gratitude the participation of my wife in my educational preparation and ministry. Today is our fifty-fifth wedding anniversary and, for us it has been, as the French say of married love, "More than yesterday and less than tomorrow."

My prayer is that God will use these articles to bless his people and to edify his church.

James M. Beaty
Professor Emeritus of New Testament
Church of God Theological Seminary
August 7, 2003

Contents

Miscellanea by the Author

Twilight

I thought---and thought---and thought---
I thought the dusk was turning into dark;
I thought I saw the twilight softly fading
    Into the shadows of night.
I feared the dark! I wished it were not so,
But now the shadows fell; I knew that soon
I'd feel a coldness in my throat.
    I did not want to go.
But sunset drove the laborers from the fields.
I did not want to say good-bye
To them who through the noonday sun
    Had toiled along with me.
How little had I thought of
What each one had meant to me!
How every one of us had worked as one--
    And now to say good-bye!
And know that this would end it all
And face alone the darkness of the night!

I thought---and thought---and thought---
And then---across the eastern rim
I saw a faded streak of light;
    I looked again.

Continued on next page.

Ah, yes, 'twas faded but not fading;
My heart leaped up---I saw that
This was twilight, but not sunset,
    I saw the shadows flee;
I saw the morning dawn,
And deep within my soul I heard again
The words the Master spoke:
    "He that follows me
    Shall not walk in darkness,
    But shall have the light of life."

And then I realized we didn't have to part---
We didn't have to say good-bye---
For always we could be united
    In purpose and in heart.
How glad I was that this was not the end,
That this was not the finish,
That yet there is a race to run.

And now we stand
Upon the threshold of another day;
The streaks of gray across the western skies
    Are not yet quite gone,
But the golden stream of sunlight from the east,
    Dispels all fear.
And with the gentle breeze that blows,
Gives assurance to each heart
That what the Master said so long ago

    Forever shall be true:
    Habebunt Lumen Vitae!

Part One

Pentecostal Experience

ESSENTIAL ELEMENTS
OF THE PENTECOSTAL FAITH [1]

As Pentecostals we need to explore and to identify the "essential elements" of the Pentecostal Faith, so that these may be protected and transmitted to future generations. The first matter at hand is to define the concept of "essential elements". In other words, what do we mean when we say that something is an essential element of something else? Do we mean that it is analogous to the oxygen in water (H_2O), that is, if the oxygen is removed, what remains is hydrogen and not water? If so, then an essential element is that without which the larger whole loses its identity. Or is an essential element to be thought of more like a member of an organic body? If so, then a distinction has to be made between that part which is essential to the life of the organism and that part which is essential to its wholeness? Or is there a third possibility, that the Pentecostal Faith is a spiritual reality, composed of essential elements, incarnate in a specific, concrete, historical context, composed of elements which are optional, cultural and historical?

I would suggest that there are dimensions of truth in all of these paradigms. There are definitely elements of Pentecostalism which are cultural manifestations and not of the essence of the faith. There are other elements which are genuine and legitimate, but not absolutely essential to its survival. And there are other elements, without which the Pentecostal Faith would

---

[1] This is a revision of an address given on January 8, 1981 to Church of God State Overseers in a retreat at the Seminary. The word "Pentecostal," as used here, reflects its context within the Church of God, not in the broader context of the "Pentecostal" movement.

be less than, and other than, what it is. But before we pursue the question of what the essential elements are, let us ask, What is the Pentecostal Faith?

We, Pentecostals, have always maintained that the Pentecostal Faith is the faith of the Apostles and the hundred and twenty who received the Pentecostal fullness on the Day of Pentecost. We have understood that the Pentecostal Faith is the New Testament faith and the faith of the early Church. That faith has continued to exist, although in a weakened and diminished form, throughout the history of the church. I am also convinced that the historic faith of the church, as expressed throughout the ages in the Apostles' Creed is integral to, but not the totality of, Pentecostal Faith, because Pentecostal Faith is more than creedal faith.

Rabbi Martin Buber in his book, *Two Types of Faith*, sets forth two paradigms: one of "faith in..." and another of "faith that..."[2] The first of these two, viz., "faith in" or trust in the living God, he sought to identify as Jewish faith and the second, viz., "faith that" or a statement of right belief and teaching, he sought to identity with Christian faith as expressed in the creeds of the Church. I believe that he gave us two useful and legitimate paradigms which can serve us well as Pentecostals, but that he failed to see that they are linked together and indeed that they are complementary. For faith in the living God demands statements of affirmations concerning God. It involves saying "Yes" to that which is true and saying "No" to that which is false.[3] And this is just as true in the Old Testament as it is in the New Testament.[4]

---

[2] Martin Buber, *Two Types of Faith* (New York: Harper and Row, 1961), 177 pp.

[3] See Karl Barth, *Credo* (New York: Charles Scribner's Sons, 1936), p. 6.

[4] **In the OT**, e.g.: The LORD is the eternal God ("from everlasting to everlasting Thou art God" Ps 90:2) and the Creator of all things ("In the beginning God created the heavens and the earth" Gn 1:1), who redeemed Israel ("I am the LORD, your God, who brought you out of the land of Egypt, out of the house of bondage" Ex 20:2) and made a covenant with

Pentecostal Faith demands, first of all, a full-orbed expression as a living faith in God, which includes walking in obedience to God, and then it demands a declaration or confession of faith which says "Yes" to Biblical truth and "sound doctrine" and which says "No" to doctrinal error and false doctrine. This may sound strange in the light of the strong opposition to "creeds" which existed in the early days of our movement. Richard Green Spurling (this is the son) was insistent in his opposition to creeds, but what he says seems to be directed primarily against creedalism, or a misuse of creeds. They were, he said, based on the "commandments of men" and resulted in having more authority than the Word. He does not envision a creed as an instrument for confessing faith in God or one for setting forth sound doctrine.

Yet as early as 1910 Spurling, along with three others, sat on a committee to draw up a list of the "Teachings Made Prominent" by the Church with supporting biblical references. This document, which was entitled, "Church of God Teachings," was produced as a guideline for those who were preparing to be examined for the ministry.[5]

---

them ("the LORD our God made a covenant with us in Horeb" Dt 5:2). He is not like the gods of the nations; He cannot be contained in a house made with hands, etc. Thus we see that there is definitely a "faith that" dimension in the Old Testament, although the scribes and rabbis lifted up and codified the commandments as expressions of obedience to "faith in" God. They called this area of teaching "Halakah" or "How to Walk/Live".

And in the NT: Likewise the faith of the New Testament finds expression as both "faith in" and "faith that". This can be illustrated from one writer, John, e.g., (1) "For God so loved the world that He gave His only begotten Son, that whosoever *believes in Him* should not perish but have everlasting life" (Jn 3:16) and (2) "These (things) are written that you may *believe that Jesus is the Christ* (i.e., the Messiah), the Son of God, and that (through) believing you may have life in His name" (Jn 20:31). In other words a "faith in" implies a "faith that"; we believe "in" one about whom we believe "that" He is the Sent One from the Father. Believing that He was or is anything less would not merit believing in Him.

[5] It is interesting that our sister organization, the Assemblies of God, had to define its doctrine of God against a form of Unitarianism which arose very

Let us now consider the early church for some guidance. The gospel which the early church proclaimed was the good news that the Eternal God, who loved us even when we were enemies, had both promised to send redemption and had acted by sending His Son to die for all as the Savior of the world, so that we might be forgiven and receive eternal life.[6] To this declaration of good news was joined the command of the Lord: repent, believe and be baptized. A person repented (turned from sin) and believed (turned to God) by turning to God in prayer, after which he or she was baptized in the name of (on the authority of) the Father, the Son and the Holy Spirit. As part of the rite of water baptism, each candidate would profess (i.e., speak forth) his or her faith or trust "in" the living God through the Lord Jesus Christ and the Holy Spirit. They were also asked to confess publicly (i.e., to speak forth with the church) its statement of belief "that" certain things about the Father, the Son and the Holy Spirit were held by the church to be true.

This process may have been at first in the form of answers to three questions: (1) "Have you placed your faith and trust in the one, true, living God?" (2) "And in Jesus Christ as Son of God and Saviour?" (3) "And in the Holy Spirit?" And this was probably reduced to the simple statement, "I believe in God the Father, in Jesus Christ and in the Holy Spirit." In the process of time appositions and "that" clauses were added and the Apostles' Creed was produced. This served as a liturgical instrument through which the church could confess, in a public and corporate act, the Christian faith as both a living faith and a statement of correct doctrine.

---

soon after they organized in 1914. Thus we see that both of these Pentecostal movements found it necessary, very early in their existence, to define the "faith that" of each movement in a formal statement.

[6] "For God so loved the world that he gave His only-begotten Son so that whosoever believes in Him should not perish but have everlasting life" (Jn 3:16).

The content of the faith (or correct doctrine) as stated in the Apostles' Creed can be summarized as follows:

　God the Father,
　　Almighty Maker of heaven and earth.
　Jesus Christ is God's Only Begotten Son and our Lord:
　　He was conceived of the Holy Spirit
　　　and born of the Virgin Mary;
　　He suffered under Pontius Pilate:
　　　He was crucified, dead and buried;
　　He descended into hell;
　　He rose from the dead on the third day.
　　He ascended into heaven:
　　He sits at the right hand of God the Father Almighty;
　　He shall come to judge the living and the dead.
　The Holy Spirit (and...)
　The Church:
　　one, holy, universal church
　　and the communion of saints
　Christian Experience:
　　the forgiveness of sins
　Christian Hope:
　　the resurrection of the body and eternal life

Apart from this baptismal profession which was turned into a confession of faith, there existed from the earliest time, what is commonly known as the *Didache* or the *Teaching*. Paul refers to this type of teaching as "How to Walk and Please God" (1 Th 4:1).[7] C. H. Dodd reconstructs the teaching from the instructions and imperatives in the epistles and the sermons in Acts. This kind of teaching has always been important where Christians have sought to love God, to do His will and to live for His glory. A life of obedience is absolutely necessary for

---

[7] C. H. Dodd, *The Apostolic Preaching, Three Lectures* (New York: Harper and Brothers, 1944), 96 pp. and *Gospel and Law* (New York: Columbia University Press, 1951), 83 pp.

the Christian believer, who by the grace of God and a faith response has become a child of the Heavenly Father, a disciple and servant of the Lord Jesus Christ and the instrument and channel of the Holy Spirit.

Later the creed was expanded to say "No" to false teachings and to say "Yes" to "sound doctrine."[8] It was out of this process of defining the position of the church and negating heresy that theology arose, resulting, it seems to me, from the interaction of two things: (1) the questioning of Greek philosophy, which had developed, to a high degree, the reasoning and ordering powers of the human mind and (2) the "faith that" statements of Scripture. This had already been intimated in the instruction of Peter, that his readers should be "ready to give an answer to everyone for the hope that is in you" (1 Pe 3:15).[9]

* * *

Now let us look at the early history of the Church of God. In the General Assembly of 1913, R. G. Spurling, Jr. preached a sermon on the church and used three charts to illustrate it. The first sets forth three things from left to right: (1) the Cross representing the doctrine of redemption; (2) the house of Christian experience: with the first, second and third floors labeled Regeneration, Sanctification and the upper room of Pentecost (i.e., the Fullness of the Holy Spirit); and (3) the foursquare city representing the Church. A path connects the Cross to the house of Christian experience, which is butted up against the walls of the Holy City or the Church. His second chart shows the harlot of the Book of the Revelation, seated on the seven-headed beast, which in his sermon is the church gone astray. The third chart depicts the Railway to Heaven on two golden rails, which Spurling interprets as the two great command-

---

[8] This became more and more important in the early church. See 1 Tim 1:10; 2 Tim 4:3; Tit 1:9; 2:1; see also 2 Tim 1:13; Tit 1:13; 2:2; 2:8.

[9] As the church drifted away from early Christian experience and the Apostles' doctrine, its errors, of course, fed into the creeds and the statements of theology which were then produced.

ments of Jesus, viz., love of God and love of neighbor. The chart shows the engine on the rails at the left of the chart. In the center there is a maize of narrow-gage rails in disorder, which represent man-made creeds. On the right of the chart the two golden rails of love protrude. The point of the sermon was the need for the church to recover its purpose, in order to made its way into the future in accordance with the will of God. Implicit in the sermon is the fact that Christian experience grows out of doctrine and is, in turn, the door of entrance into the Christian life, i.e., participation in the life of the church.

In 1910 the August 15 issue of the *Evangel*, the first issue of which had appeared in March of that year, was dedicated to the doctrines of the Church of God. A list, entitled Church of God Teachings, which was the work of a committee composed of M. S. Lemons, R. G. Spurling, Jr., T. L McLain and A. J. Tomlinson, was published in that issue of the *Evangel*. It was prefaced by these words:

TEACHINGS
The Church of God stands for the whole Bible rightly divided. The New Testament is the only rule for government and discipline.

These teachings say nothing about the Bible, the Doctrine of God (Trinity), the Person and Work of Jesus Christ, the Doctrine of the Holy Spirit, the Church, etc., i.e., the whole range of Christian Theology. But rather they are centered on Christian experience, the Christian life and the Christian hope. I had always assumed that the list had no particular organization; and I have never heard this assumption questioned. But in this present study I asked myself if there could possibly be some order in the arrangement of this document; and it appears that the twenty-five numbered items of teaching fall into two sections consisting of four parts in each, as follows:

A. Pentecostal Experience:
Beginning the Christian Life.
I.Conversion (Salvation or Getting Saved)
Repentance - Mk 1:15; Lk 13:3; Ac 3:19
Justification - Rom 5:1; Tit 3:7
Regeneration - Tit 3:5
New Birth - Jn 3:3; 1 Pe 1:23; 1 Jn 3:9
2. Sanctification subsequent to Justification
Rom 5:2; 1 Cor 1:30; 1 Th 4:3; Heb 13:12
Holiness - Lk 1:75; 1 Th 4:7; Heb 12:14
3. Water Baptism - Mt 28:19; Mk 1:9f; Jn 3:22f; Ac 8:36, 38
4. Baptism in the Holy Spirit subsequent to cleansing:
the enduement of power for service.
Mt 3:11; Lk 24:49, 53; Ac 1:4-8
The Speaking in Tongues as the Spirit gives utterance
as the initial evidence of the baptism of the Holy Ghost.
Jn 15:16; Ac 2:4; 10:44ff; 19:1-7

B. Pentecostal Spirituality:
Continuing the Christian Life
Inner Dimensions
1. Spiritual Gifts
1 Cor 12:1, 7-10, 28, 31; 14:1
2. Signs following believers
Mk 16:17-20; Rom 15:18f; Heb 2:4
3. Fruit of the Spirit
Rom 6:22; Gal 5:22f; Eph 5:9; Phl 1:11
4. Divine Healing
provided for all in the atonement
Ps 103:3; Is 53:4f; Mt 8:17; Jas 5:14-16; 1 Pe 2:24
Outward Aspects
1. The Lord's Supper
Lk 22:17-20; 1 Cor 11:23-26
2. Washing the saints' feet
Jn 13:4-17; 1 Tim 5:9f
3. Tithing and Giving
Gn 14:18-20; 28:20ff; Mal 3:10;
Lk 11:42; 1 Cor 9:6-9; 16:2; Heb 7:1-21
4. Restitution where possible
Mt 3:8; Lk 19:8f

C. The Christian Hope and the End
1. Premillennial second coming of Jesus.
   a. First, to resurrect the dead saints
      and to catch away the living saints
      to Him in the air.
      1 Cor 15:32; 1 Th 4:15ff; 2 Th 2:1
   b. Second, to reign on the earth
      a thousand years.
      Zech 14:4; 1 Th 4:14; 2 Th 1:7-10; Jude 14f;
      Rev 5:10; 19:11-21; 20:4-6
2. Resurrection
   Jn 5:28f; Ac 24:15; Rev 20:5f
3. Eternal life for the righteous.
   Mt 25:46; Lk 18:30; Jn 10:28; Rom 6:22;
   1 Jn 5:11ff
4. Eternal punishment for the wicked.
   No liberation nor annihilation.
   Mt 25:41-46; Mk 3:29; 2 Th 1:8f; Rev 20:10-15; 21:8

D. Some Practical Commitments[10]
   1. Total abstinence from all liquor or strong drinks
      Prov 20:1; 23:29-32; Isa 28:7; 1 Cor 5:11; 6:10; Gal 5:21
   2. Against the use of tobacco in any form,
      opium, morphine, etc.
      Isa 55:2; 1 Cor 10:31f; 2 Cor 7:1; Eph 5:3-8; Jas 1:21
   3. Meats and drinks
      Rom 14:2-17; 1 Cor 8:8; 1 Tim 4:1-5
   4. The Sabbath
      Hos 2:11; Rom 14:5f; Col 2:16f; Rom 13:1f[11]

The Declaration of Faith was put together in 1948 in Birmingham by the following committee, which was called the "Articles of Faith Committee": James L. Slay, Chairman, Earl

---

[10] These were revised and incorporated into the new document on the Practical Commitments adopted by the 62nd General Assembly in 1988. See Minutes 1988, p, 51.

[11] A brief and simple commentary on this list of teachings is appended to this chapter.

P. Paulk, Sr., Glenn C. Pettyjohn, J. L. Goins, James A. Cross, R. P. Johnson, R. C. Muncy, and E. M. Ellis.[12] According to the chairman, the work on the Declaration of Faith was done in "my hotel room at the Moulton Hotel in Birmingham. We had no other information but what was in our heads."[13] The document which they prepared consisted of a bringing together and slightly amplifying most of the 1910 Teachings (the so-called practical commitments were felt to be of a different order, apparently) with the addition of three items: (1) an article on the verbal inspiration of the Bible, (2) an article on the Trinity and (3) and an article on Jesus Christ. All three of these are influenced by the Declaration of Faith of the National Association of Evangelicals, which had been adopted in 1943 in Chicago (Earl P. Paulk, Sr. was one of the Church of God delegates at that meeting). And the third article of both Declarations is almost word-for-word from the Apostles' Creed. And the addition of the word, bodily, before resurrection in article 14 is an echo of the phrase 'the resurrection of the body' in the Apostles' Creed.

* * *

Now for some conclusions: What are the essential elements of the Pentecostal faith? My conclusions are:
1. The Verbal Inspiration of the Bible.
   (Without this we shall loose our mooring.)
2. The Doctrine of the Trinity.
3. The Divinity and Humanity of Jesus Christ.
4 The Incorporating Experiences:
   Salvation, Sanctification,
   Water Baptism
   and Baptism in the Holy Spirit.
5. Living the Life:
   The Cultivation of Pentecostal Spirituality,
   both inner and outer aspects

---

[12] See 1948 General Assembly Minutes, p.31.
[13] From a letter by James L. Slay to the author; now in the Pentecostal Research Center in Cleveland, Tennessee.

(emphasizing prayer and reading of the Word)[14]
balancing hope (and service)
as we live holy lives.
6. (The Church as called to be one, holy, apostolic, and
   universal church.)

When this paper was first delivered, the Church of God had never made an official statement on the church.[15] However, our history has emphasized it. The name "Christian Union" emphasized the fact that the church is called to be one; the name "Holiness Church," that the church is called to be holy; the name, "Church of God," that the church is called to be apostolic; and the missionary thrust, resulting from the baptism in the Holy Spirit, that the church is called to be an international and universal church.

Our mandate, as I hear it from the Word and from the Spirit, is to live the life and to proclaim the Word. Nothing else will cause others to receive the Word and make it a part of their lives.[16]

---

[14] The words in the three sets of parentheses summarize from Scripture what is not specified in the church documents, but understood by the members.

[15] A statement of the church was adopted in 1998. See Minutes, p. 51).

[16] See 1 Th 1:6-8 (note the sequence): (1) receive the Word, (2) become imitators, (3) become examples, and (4) sound forth the Word.

A Brief Commentary on the Teachings

Let us look briefly at the Teachings in the light of the outline proposed in this chapter.

PENTECOSTAL EXPERIENCE

Beginning the Christian Life

I. Repentance and the New Birth

The first teaching is just one word, "Repentance." But the meaning is clearly that of the latter-amplified statement in the Declaration of Faith (1948): 4. "That all have sinned and come short of the glory of God and that repentance is commanded of God for all and necessary for forgiveness of sins." This is the gospel command, "Repent and believe"; for the two always go together, or maybe we should say that one is always incomplete without the other. When the Word comes in the power of the Spirit, commanding the hearer to turn "to God from idols" (1 Th 1:9), if the heart is willing, faith turns to God; repentance turns from idols, but both are part of the same turning. The conviction of the Holy Spirit brings sorrow for sin. This was such a reality in the early days of the church, that "dry-eyed" repentance was not trusted.

The lifting of the burden of condemnation and the forgiveness of sins result in "Justification" and "Regeneration" or "New Birth." These are all biblical terms referring to different aspects of salvation or conversion. Justification is a legal term and a favorite word of the Apostle Paul. It refers to vindication at the bar of justice, due to the price already paid by Jesus Christ; and it means, as Paul states, that "there is therefore now no condemnation" (Rom 8:1).

Regeneration and New Birth are, respectively, the Latin and the Anglo-Saxon terms for the same thing, viz., receiving eternal life. Whoever believes (trusts in the Lord) is made a new creature, is born of the Spirit, receives eternal life and becomes a son or daughter of the Heavenly Father. As later expanded in the Declaration of Faith, We believe "That justification, regeneration and the new birth are wrought by faith in the blood of Jesus Christ." Thus we see that Christian experience is based on the doctrine of the atoning death and sacrifice of Jesus Christ.

II. Sanctification

Again we have a linguistic consideration, viz., that sanctification and holiness in English use different stems, again from Latin and Anglo-Saxon, to talk about things in the same area. The intention of each is amplified in the Declaration of Faith:

6. We believe in sanctification
   subsequent to the new birth,
   through faith in the blood of Christ,
   through the Word, and by the Holy Ghost.
7. We believe holiness to be
   God's standard of living for His people.

As far as I can tell, the 1910 teachings on Sanctification and Holiness are based squarely on Wesleyan teaching, which reached the members of the committee through the Holiness Movement.[17] However, by 1948 when the Declaration of Faith was adapted there was, according to a letter received from the chairman of the committee, James L. Slay, a strong difference of opinion as to whether sanctification was a second, definite experience or not.

---

[17] Tomlinson was converted in a "Quaker-Holiness" meeting and was influenced by God's Bible School in Cincinnati, an institution of the holiness movement, and by "God's Revivalist," edited there by M.W. Knapp. Both Spurling, first a Baptist and then a collaorator of the Methodists, and Bryant were influenced by the ministers of the revival of 1896 in Shearer Schoolhouse, who were influenced by the Fire-baptized Movement.

But the first believers in the mountains had experienced the holiness revival; they had come into the experience of sanctification after being converted. Through sanctification they had experienced: (1) deliverance from bondage and habits which had persisted after they were converted or saved and (2) a full, deep and abiding joy. The experience and the lifestyle which followed had won for each of them the label of "old sanky" (from sanctified). For my part, I believe that they did indeed receive a true understanding from God, and that is, that the eternal, holy God can break the fetters that bind the human soul and release one into the "glorious liberty" of the children of God, where the Christian life can be lived in its abundance with victory and joy.

III. Water Baptism

The order of the Teachings at this point almost seems to be an echo of the words of Peter on the Day of Pentecost, "Repent and be baptized... and you shall receive the gift of the Holy Spirit" [Ac 2:38], since in both instances water baptism is placed after repentance and before reception of the Holy Spirit. The listing in the Evangel had read "Water Baptism by immersion", but in the following Assembly "by immersion" was dropped, not because there was any quarrel about the mode of baptism, but because the terminology itself was not found in Scripture. However, this was later reinserted; and the Trinitarian formula of Mt 28:19 was specified in Article No. 10 of the Declaration of Faith, which reads, "We believe in water baptism by immersion, and all who repent should be baptized in the name of the Father, and of the Son, and of the Holy Ghost."

IV. Baptism in the Holy Spirit

First, two words about terminology: (1) it seems to me that we would do well to standardize our terminology as "baptized in the Holy Spirit" (not *of* or *with*) since this both follows the explicit Greek terminology in the words of John the Baptist and

Jesus and best fits the contrast of baptism "in" water, which John also uses and (2) the term, Holy Spirit, is, of course, the same as Holy Ghost, which was an archaic term even in 1611, when the King James Version was published. Elsewhere in the KJV we always find "the Spirit" and "the Spirit of God", never the "Ghost" or "the Ghost of God".

In the two Teachings that follow, viz., No. 8 and No. 9, the Baptism in the Holy Spirit is set forth as (1) the enduement of power (i.e., being clothed or invested with power), (2) as subsequent to cleansing, and (3) according to Ac 2:4, with the evidence (sign) of speaking in tongues as the Spirit gives the utterance. This is the cardinal doctrine of the Pentecostal Movement and the keystone of the Pentecostal faith. If this experience and this doctrine are ever lost, the Church of God will be a different church and the Pentecostal Movement will be a different movement.

PENTECOSTAL SPIRITUALITY

Continuing the Christian Life

Up through No. 9, the Teachings address the beginnings of the spiritual life. No. 10 and following address the continuation of the Christian Life, in terms of Pentecostal Spirituality.

I. The Inner Reality of Pentecostal Spirituality

The exercise of spiritual gifts is the hallmark of Pentecostalism and the most distinctive feature of Pentecostal worship. "Signs Following" should be expected as the confirming act of God in Pentecostal evangelism and missions (Mk 16:20). The fruit of the Spirit is what the Spirit does *in* us, as He molds us into the likeness of Jesus Christ. This must always be a primary concern for all Pentecostals. Sometimes this can be lost sight of, as it was in Corinth, in our preoccupation with the gifts of the Spirit, understood as what the Spirit does *through* us.

Divine healing in not the same as faith healing or mental healing. As the terminology indicates, God is the healer and He gets the glory. This teaching affirms that divine healing is provided for all in the atonement. Just as salvation is provided for all, so is healing. And just because we do not see every person for whom we pray healed, we must not set aside belief in divine healing. God does not change and He is sovereign. Prayer for the sick gives God the opportunity to work miracles of divine healing in our midst and must always have a place among us.

II. Some Outward Aspects of Pentecostal Spirituality

Just as water baptism is the sacrament of initiation into the Christian faith and the means of pledging allegiance and loyalty to the Lord and His people, so the Lord's Supper and the washing of the saints' feet are ongoing sacraments of the Christian life and the means by which one renews one's covenant with, and commitment to, God and His people.

While tithing and giving are not made legalistically binding for membership in the Church of God, they are not optional in the Christian life. These acts of giving are a solemn and sacred recognition of the sovereignty of God over the life of the Christian. It is recognition, as the Word says, that "All things come from Thee, and of Thine own we have given to Thee" (1 Chr. 29:14).

Restitution speaks of making things right, whenever and wherever possible. At first, it could appear that this teaching is misplaced and that it should follow Repentance; because, when people are really under conviction, making restitution is part of their repentance and making things right with God. Years ago, it was not unusual for a person to get up from the altar, converted, and go to someone to make restitution. All of this is true, but the position of this teaching points even further. All through our Christian walk and warfare, there are moments when we have to make things right. It is another sign that Jesus Christ is Lord and that we are His servants.

III. The Christian Hope and the End

Teachings 18-21 tell us that Jesus is coming and that when He comes, we, God's People, the dead and the living, shall be resurrected and caught up to be with Him. Then the groaning of creation in us will be over and we shall enjoy eternal life forever. In the meantime, we must remember that we have been saved to serve the true and living God and to wait for his Son from heaven (1 Th 1:9f). In love we serve, but we need hope to inspire us in our serving.

These four teachings also echo the second half of Jn 3:16, "that whosoever believeth in Him should not perish but have everlasting life." Thus they also remind us that there are two eternal destinies: eternal life or eternal punishment.

IV. The Practical Commitments

The last four items of the 1910 list were, in recent years, given the name of "practical commitments." They were expanded little by little until there were thirteen (13) items and they were replaced by the new document on Practical Commitments. The original four are listed above in the outline.

The first two of these are prohibitions against the use of alcohol and the use of tobacco and drugs. These have been a part of the consensus of the Church of God from the earliest days. When the Church took a stand on these issues, it was not that popular among other Christians, and almost no data on the human destructiveness of these things existed. Today alcohol and drugs, including tobacco, are two of the most destructive problems facing society.

The last two teachings in this list were, and are, anti-Adventist. They were short and cryptic and not really clear to an outsider, although all of us on the inside knew that we were not bound by dietary laws about meats and drinks and that we did not observe Saturday as the Sabbath. Both of these had to do with Christian liberty and negating the binding power of the old covenant for believers today who live under the new covenant.

These two teachings were expanded and elaborated in 1966, after the leaders of the Church of God in South America suggested it.[18] Later this whole section was absorbed into the new document on the Practical Commitments.

---

[18] This was done in the first retreat of Overseers and leaders in South America in January of 1966 at San Bernadino, Paraguay.

ഇ ✿ ൙

BAPTISM IN THE HOLY SPIRIT [1]
Receiving the Holy Spirit

"If the baptism in the Holy Spirit were for Christians today, why is it not mentioned in the Gospels?" This is a question sometimes asked, but it is based on a certain kind of blindness, because it is precisely in the gospels, all four of them in fact, that we first find the words "baptize in the Holy Spirit." They are the words of John the Baptist: "I baptize in water, He (Christ) will baptize in the Holy Spirit."[2] This already tells us that there is a difference between baptism in water and baptism in the Holy Spirit and that baptism in the Spirit comes after baptism in water.

A

When Paul came to Ephesus, he found twelve disciples. I believe that they were disciples of John the Baptist; although at that time, John had been dead for at least twenty years. But the main interpretation of this passage does not depend on identifying them and determining if they were or were not Christians when Paul first met them. From the text we see that Paul did four things: (1) he opened the Word to them, (2) he became convinced, apparently, by their response to the Word, that they were ready to receive Christian baptism in water, (3) he baptized them in water, and (4) only then did he lay his hands on them and pray for them; and they received the fullness of the Spirit and spoke in tongues and prophesied.

---

[1] Revised from a brochure prepared for Westmore Church of God.
[2] Mt 3:11; Mk 1:8; Lk 3:16; Jn 1:33; Ac 1:5; 11:16.

Whether they were already Christian believers and then received the Holy Spirit after Paul baptized them and prayed for
them, or whether they were not Christian believers and received Christ as their Savior, were baptized in water and then
received the Holy Spirit in His fullness, does not affect our
conclusion. In either case the Baptism in the Holy Spirit, for
them, was subsequent to the new birth. So the old tension over
the translation "when or after you believed," does not make
any difference as to doctrine.

The words of Jesus in the Gospel of John about sending another Comforter implies this same difference and also implies
that the one comes after the other, as do the words of Jesus that
the spirit would be the "comforter, whom the world cannot receive" (Jn 14:15-17). In other words, the fullness of the Spirit
is for those who have already received Jesus as Savior and
Lord.

The hope, under the old covenant, was that the coming one
would pour out the Spirit in a special way. But it was not until
John, still under the old covenant, that the term "baptized" was
introduced into Scripture.[3] And the parallel between water and
Spirit has a tendency to lead one to think of the Spirit as "it,"
corresponding to the water. And this misconception is often
carried over into the expression "Receive the Holy Spirit."

But the verb "receive" has both an impersonal and a personal
meaning. We receive a letter or a gift by taking it into our
hands, and what is received, in this sense, is an "it." Since the
Holy Spirit is also referred to, especially in the *Acts of the
Apostles*, as a gift, there is a tendency for some to think of the
Holy Spirit as an "it." But if people come and knock at our
door, we "receive" them. And this has another meaning. If we
knew they were coming, we were expecting them. Or if we did
not, so much more the pleasant surprise. But how do we re-

---

[3] The rabbis had already introduced the term in connection with the proce-
dure for receiving pagan converts.

ceive our guests? We open the door, invite them in, and give them a welcome. We treat them with respect; we listen to what they say; we talk with them, and we offer them hospitality and try to serve them. So it is with the baptism in the Holy Spirit.

B

In the early days of the Pentecostal movement, a lot was heard about "tarrying" for the Holy Spirit. This was based on what Jesus told the disciples in Acts chapter one. They tarried ten days (according to most interpretations), and then the Holy Spirit came in power and they were all filled with the Holy Spirit and began to speak in tongues. That day Peter explained that the risen Christ had ascended to the Father and that Christ, after having received the promise of the Spirit, had poured out what those present "saw and heard." The tarrying in that case is clearly defined as waiting for Christ to "pour out." The "pouring out" depended on two things: (1) Christ receiving the promise from the Father and (2) the divine will that the "pouring out" correspond with the Day of Pentecost. But since the Day of Pentecost, these two things are not a factor. Now, when Jesus saves us, He is ready and willing to sanctify us, that is, break all the shackles of sin and all bondage to former habits, and to baptize us in the Holy Spirit. He who ever lives to save, also lives to sanctify and baptize in the Holy Spirit (cf. Heb 7:23-25). Therefore the "tarrying" now is not waiting for God to get ready but waiting for us to get ready.

Some people think that God has marked a day on the calendar to baptize them in the Holy Spirit and that when that day comes it will happen automatically. No! This is not how it is. God is ready at any time that we are ready.

Others, perhaps from seeing what they thought was the "flesh" or "wild fire," have said, "When I speak in tongues, it will be all of God and nothing on my part." But listen to Ac 2:4 (the golden text of Pentecost): "And they were all filled with the Holy Spirit and began to speak in other tongues as the

Spirit gave the utterance." Luke tells us two things in this sentence: (1) "They were all filled with the Holy Spirit" and (2) "They all began to speak in tongues." "They" means "each one." "Each one was filled" is passive, and Jesus, who is the Baptizer, is the one who is baptizing. But also, and apparently at the same time, "each one" began to speak. But how? "As the Spirit gave the utterance (or enablement)." The Spirit was giving and they were speaking. Speaking in tongues, like all the activities of the Spirit, depends on yieldedness, sensitivity and obedience to the Spirit. We can obey the Spirit or we can quench the Spirit, that is, not cooperate with the Spirit. Speaking in tongues is the indication that the Holy Spirit has come in fullness; and is the sign that we are sensitive and obedient and cooperating with the Holy Spirit. Scripture says that the Holy Spirit is given "to those who obey" (Ac 5:32).

Remember in your seeking, that you are not waiting on God in the sense of waiting for God to get ready. You are waiting on God in the sense of being in His presence and continuing in His presence. And this time is a time to make things right with God and to ask for God, through His Holy Spirit, to break every bond and every hindrance in your life. Remember "the promise is for you and for your children and all that are afar off, even as many as the Lord our God shall call" (Ac 2:39). A promise must be received by faith. Open your heart and receive. When the Holy Spirit comes in, he will witness and you will speak in tongues. You do not seek tongues, you seek the Lord and open yourself to the Holy Spirit.

The Baptism in the Holy Spirit in the Book of Acts
based on a Bookmark by David L. Lemons

Five Case Studies

1. Passage: **Acts 2:4**

Place and time	Jerusalem, Pentecost, AD 29
Who Received	120 Disciples
Who Ministered	Peter in Charge
Circumstances	Tarried, praising God (Lk 24:53)
Terminology	Filled with the Holy Spirit
Sign/Evidence	Spoke in tongues

2. Passage: **Acts 8:17**

Place and time	Samaria, AD 35
Who Received	Samaritans
Who Ministered	Peter and John
Circumstances	Laying on of Hands
Terminology	Received the Holy Spirit
Sign/Evidence	What motivated Simon?

3. Passage   **Acts 9:17**

Place and time	Damascus, AD 37
Who Received	Saul of Tarsus
Who Ministered	Ananias
Circumstances	Laying on of Hands
Terminology	Be filled with the Holy Spirit
Sign/Evidence	Spoke in Tongues (1 Cor 14:18)

4.Passage   **Acts 10:44**

Place and time	Caesarea, AD 41
Who Received	House of Cornelius
Who Ministered	Peter
Circumstances	Hearing of Faith
Terminology	Holy Spirit fell on all who heard
Sign/Evidence	Spoke in tongues

5. Passage **Acts 19:6**
    Place and time   Ephesus, AD 54
    Who Received   Twelve Jews
    Who Ministered   Paul
    Circumstances   Laying on of Hands
    Terminology   Holy Spirit came upon them
    Sign/Evidence   Spoke in tongues and prophesied

&) ✿ ౧౩

THE NATURE OF SPIRITUAL GIFTS [1]

The Purpose of This Paper

The purpose of this paper is to explore the interaction of the Holy Spirit and the human spirit in the operation of the spiritual gifts, in order to see if there is any pattern in this interrelationship that is rooted on the one side in the nature of the Holy Spirit and on the other in human nature. It is being suggested that the dominant principle involved in this relationship of the Holy Spirit and the human spirit is found in Ac 2:4, viz., "they spoke...as...the Spirit gave," and that this principle, in general, sets the parameters of many relationships between God and us, as human beings, and, does, specifically, characterize all manifestations of the Holy Spirit in spiritual gifts.

I

To begin, let us look at some background and seek to understand how spirits, other than the Spirit of God, relate to human beings. My own presuppositions which I bring to this study are, that there is a difference between God, as uncreated Spirit, and all "spirits" and "spiritual" creatures. In the non-physical realm of created spirit being, there are spirits who are obedient and others who are disobedient to the Eternal Creator. This means that a person may be confronted with, and have communication with, three different kinds of spirit beings: (1) created and obedient spirit beings, (2) created and disobedient spirit beings, and (3) the uncreated Spirit of the Almighty Himself.

---

[1] The original draft of this paper was read at the Annual Meeting of the Society for Pentecostal Studies at Fuller Theological Seminary in Pasadena, CA on November 20, 1982.

The first group are obedient servants of the Most High and serve both in the Old Testament and, to some extent, in the New as Messengers of God to specific people. When these ministering spirits appear, the first word spoken is generally, "Fear not," and then God's message is respectfully communicated. In general, their sudden appearance and disappearance, along with other phenomena, make one aware that this is a visit of a spirit being. However, Scripture also speaks of those who have "entertained angels unawares" (Heb 13:2).

It is clear from both Scripture and history that created, disobedient spirit beings have been in communication with human beings from earliest times. These rebellious spirit beings have sought to alienate human beings from the Eternal Creator, to usurp His prerogatives and thereby to bring His creatures under alien servitude. They communicate with human beings in two principal ways. From without they insinuate thoughts into the mind; Paul calls these "flaming darts of the evil one" (Eph 6:16). These affect the "imagination of the thoughts of the heart" (Gen 6:5) and, if not rejected, produce evil thoughts, evil desires and evil acts.

The second way that evil spirits communicate with men and women is that they violate and invade the human psyche, turn off the human personality and usurp the human faculties for their own ends. This may be temporary as in the experience of the medium, for purposes of communication and deception, or more or less permanent, as in the case of those who are demon possessed.

In the matter of insinuating thoughts, the way the Holy Spirit and evil spirits operate appears to be very similar, but the end, in each case, is opposite, viz., destruction and death on the one hand and blessing and life on the other. But in the other case of more intimate communication, the way the Holy Spirit relates to a person and the way an evil spirit relates are diametrically opposed. To illuminate this, it is most instructive to understand how the evil spirit relates to a human being, especially in that dimension of speaking through him.

Plato, when speaking of the popular belief that the liver is the seat of divination, recognized this and wrote:

Herein is a proof that God has given the art of divination (foretelling) not to the wisdom but to the foolishness of man. No man, when in his wits, attains prophetic truth and inspiration: but when he receives the inspired word, either his intelligence is enthralled in sleep, or he is demented by some distemper or possession.[2]

In the Old Testament Israel is forbidden to consult with evil spirits.[3] One of the more explicit prohibitions occurs in Dt 18:9-14:

When you come into the land
which the LORD your God gives you,
you shall not learn to follow
the abominable practices of those nations.
There shall not be found among you any one
who burns his son or his daughter as an offering,
any one who practices divination, a soothsayer,
or an augur, or a sorcerer, or a charmer,
or a medium, or a wizard, or a necromancer.
For whoever does these things
is an abomination to the LORD;
and because of these abominable practices
the LORD your God is driving them out before you.
You shall be blameless before the LORD your God.
For these nations, which you are about to dispossess,
give heed to soothsayers and to diviners;
but as for you,
the LORD your God has not allowed you so to do.

---

[2] Plato (*Timaeus* 71a), tr by Jowetts, cited by Richard Rackham, *The Acts of the Apostles* (London: Methuen, 1957), p. 20.
[3] Lv 19:31, 20:6,27; Dt 18:9-14; 2 Kings 21:6; cf. Isa 8:19 and 1 Sam 28:5-25.

It is interesting to note that this whole chapter deals with communicating with the spirit world. In Scripture, the worship of the LORD is the only authorized traffic with the spirit world. Accordingly, in the first eight verses instructions are given concerning the Levitical priests who are chosen "to stand and minister in the name of the LORD" (v 5). And following the prohibition Israel is given the promise of the prophet like unto Moses, of whom the LORD said, "I will put my words in his mouth, and he shall speak to them all that I command him" (v 18). Then follows a warning on the dangers of being a false prophet, i.e., one "who presumes to speak a word in my name which I have not commanded him to speak" (v 20).

Since the act of consulting spirits is forbidden in Scripture, there is not a lot of evidence about the state of the "medium" during this process of communication, although such communication is recognized. At Philippi Paul encountered "a slave girl who had a spirit of divination" who through soothsaying brought gain to her owners. When Paul cast the spirit out of her in the name of Jesus Christ, "her owners saw that their hope of gain was gone" (Ac 16:16-19).

Passing from the "medium" to the "demon-possessed," it is quite clear in Scripture that such persons are dispossessed of their own faculties and equally clear that once the demonic spirit is gone, they return to their normal state. The Gadarene, once delivered, is said to have been "in his right mind" (Mk 5:15; Lk 9:35).

At this point it is instructive to note what Paul had to say in his "Preamble to Spiritual Gifts" in 1 Cor 12:1-3.[4]
> Now in reference to Spiritual Gifts, brothers and sisters,
> I do not want you to misunderstand.
> You know that when you were heathen,

---

[4] Translation of 1 Cor 12:1-3 is by the author.

you were led away as prisoners[5] unto dumb idols,
as if you were taken into custody.[6]

Here Paul is saying that if one is misinformed about these
things, one can be misled, even by one's own mind. He did not
want them to draw false conclusions and inept comparisons
between what they knew about the activity of spirits as pagans
and the activity of God's Holy Spirit, who glorifies Jesus and
without whom no one comes to know Jesus as Lord.

The emphasis here is, from the human side, on the involuntary
aspect of this communication with the spirit world. This is
bondage; this is slavery. In reference the words, 'to lead and to
lead astray' (*agein...apagein*), Conzelmann says,

> The significance of the words allows of no certain conclu-
> sion. The phrase certainly implies that they were not their
> own masters; but this can just as well mean being domi-
> nated in a general way by demons, the actors in the pagan
> cult (see 8:1-6; 10:20), as being swept into ecstasy.[7]

Conzelmann also says that the acclamation, 'Jesus is Lord', is
not a "possibility proper to man. But in contradistinction to
Gnosticism and normal ecstasy, *the subject is not extinguished
by the Spirit* (emphasis mine)--a point which Paul brings out in
chap. 14."[8] He t cites Weiss, in connection with this passage:

> Here (in 1 Cor 12:1-3) the intention is not to emphasize a
> distinction from paganism, but an analogy; you know of
> course from your own experience how a man has no will of
> his own when he is in the power of the πνεῦμα (Spirit).

[5] Walter Bauer, William F. Arndt and F. Wilbur Gringich, *A Greek-English Lexicon of the New Testament and other early Christian literature* (Chicago: University of Chicago Press, 1957), p. 78: "ἀπάγω (a-PAH-go), 2.b. *lead away* a prisoner or condemned man."

[6] Ibid., p. 14: "ἄγω (AH-go), 2. legal t.t., *lead away, take into* custody." 206

[7] Hans Conzelman, *1 Corinthians* (Philadelphia: Fortress, 1975), p.205.

[8] Ibid., p. 206, n.21.

Thus the whole question is concerned only with ecstatics, not with men in a normal condition.[9]

What I am arguing in this paper is that Paul is making a contrast between the pagan and the Christian approach to dealing with the spirit world. Pagan ecstasy involves an involuntary take-over by the spirit, whereas the Christian experience of being filled with the Spirit and the exercise of spiritual gifts involve sensitivity, obedience, cooperation and control.

Now to return to Paul, he proceeds to lay out two guidelines or principles which relate to the Spirit and to Jesus as Lord.

First, "No one who speaks by the Spirit of God says, 'Jesus is anathema'" (1 Cor 12:3). This is a statement against the self-sufficiency, independence, and autonomy of any spirit over against Jesus the Lord, Who can neither be belittled nor ignored. The true Spirit is the Spirit of Jesus, and the purpose of the Spirit is to glorify Jesus. In other words, there is "NO SPIRIT WITHOUT JESUS."

Second, "No one can say 'Jesus is Lord,' except by the Holy Spirit" (1 Cor 12:3). Thus we see that the Spirit links us to Jesus. By one single Spirit we are baptized into (joined to—placed into) one body (1 Cor 12:13). We are born of the Spirit, raised to new life by the Spirit. So there is "NO JESUS WITHOUT THE SPIRIT."

In order to demonstrate what is really involved in pagan possession, the following experience of the late Maya Deren is cited from her book. *Divine Horsemen: Voodoo Gods of Haiti.*[10] Miss Deren was born in Russia, the daughter of a psychiatrist and was, to quote the dust-jacket of her book, "a pioneer in developing the non-fiction film beyond the traditional limits of the documentary." In 1947 she went to Haiti to study

---

[9] Ibid., p. 206..

[10] Maya Deren, *Divine Horsemen, Voodoo Gods of Haiti* (New York: Chelsea House, 1970).

and record the Haitian dance. In looking for the significance of the dance, she got involved in Voodoo, and this led her into the experience of being "mounted" (or possessed) by a Voodoo *loa* (or spirit). In Haitian culture this is the way the experience is described; and this is her explanation for the title of her book.

The setting is a "peristyle," which is an open-sided, rectangular building with a dirt floor and a tin roof. The wall of one end and the two sides of the building is three feet high, but at the other end it goes up to the roof. Standing near that wall, three drummers are pounding on three drums of different sizes at a deadening volume. About twenty people are dancing around the "middle post", which is understood to be the pathway of descent for the spirits. Each person is dancing individually invoking Erzulie, a female Voodoo *loa*. Deren is participating and describes the "rhythm" of the dance and what happened in the following way:

> The pace which had seemed unbearably demanding had slipped down a notch into a slow-motion, so that my mind had time, now, to wander, to observe at leisure, what a splendid thing it was, indeed, to hear the drums, to move like this, to be able to do all this so easily....

As sometimes in dreams, so here I can observe myself, can note with pleasure how the full hem of my white skirt plays with the rhythms, can watch, as if in a mirror, how the smile begins with a softening of the lips, spreads unperceptibly into a radiance which, surely, is lovelier than any I have ever seen. It is when I turn, as if to a neighbor, to say, "Look! See how lovely it is!" and see that the others are removed to a distance, withdrawn to a circle which is already watching, that I realize, like a shaft of terror struck through me, that it is no longer myself whom I watch. Yet it *is* myself. for as that terror strikes, we two are made one again, joined by and upon the point of the left leg which is rooted to the earth. Now there is only terror. "This is it!" Resting upon that leg I feel a strange numbness enter it from the earth itself and mount, within the very marrow of the bone, as slowly and richly as sap might mount the trunk of a tree. I say numbness, but that is inaccurate. To be precise, I must say what, even to me, is pure recollection, but not otherwise conceivable: I must call it a white darkness, its whiteness a glory and its darkness, terror.....

I cannot wrench the leg free. I am caught in this cylinder, this well of sound. There is nothing anywhere except this. There is no way out. The white darkness moves up the veins of my legs like a swift tide rising, rising; it is a great force which I cannot sustain or contain, which, surely, will burst my skin. It is too much, too bright, too white for me; this is its darkness. "Mercy!" I scream within me. I hear it echoed by the voices, shrill and unearthly: "Erzulie!" The bright darkness floods up through my body, reaches my head, engulfs me. I am sucked down and exploded upward at once. That is all.[11]

This is Maya Deren's description of her own experience. In reflecting on it, she makes some observations which I shall now cite to show the two major points of difference between pagan possession and the Christian experience of the Spirit.

1. The Holy Spirit respects the human person, as well as one's freedom, one's willingness and one's integrity. Other spirits do not, but violate, invade, usurp and use the human person. In contrasting hypnosis and possession. Miss Deren declares that the former is "dependent upon relaxation and agreement," whereas "possession takes place in spite of the most active resistance engendered by terror."[12]

2. The second point of contrast focuses on the state of the person under the influence of the spirit. In the case of the Holy Spirit, the person retains awareness (i.e., inner awareness) and freedom (i.e., to cooperate or not to cooperate). In the case of other spirits, awareness (consciousness) and freedom are surrendered.

---

[11] Ibid., pp. 258-60.
[12] Ibid., p.321, n.5.

In later reflections Miss Deren confirmed this in two very clear-cut statements: (1) "the self must leave if the loa is to enter,"[13] and (2) "the period during which the loa was 'installed' is a complete blank in my memory."[14]

The Holy Spirit is gentle and seeks cooperation, yieldedness and obedience, and does not violate our personhood or "switch us off." The person in whom the Spirit works must be sensitive to the will of the Spirit and then respond in willing obedience.

We Pentecostals used to say concerning certain experiences that so-and-so was "out under the power." But they awee "out" only in reference to what was going on around them. They maintain consciousness within themselves and were aware of what they were experiencing spiritually, which may have been visions, revelations, or overwhelming joy. And when the experience is over, it is never the case that the memory is left a complete blank.

II

Now let us look at how the uncreated Spirit of the Almighty, Himself, relates to the believer. In my exegesis (and interpretation) of Ac 2:2-4, I have come to see three simultaneous and logically distinct events in the outpouring of the Holy Spirit on the Day of Pentecost. In v 2, there is the coming of the Holy Spirit; in v 3, there is the constitution of the Church (this was accomplished by joining all the believers by the same Spirit to Jesus Christ and to each other); and in v 4, there is the baptism in the Holy Spirit, as promised earlier (Lk 24:49; Ac 1:5,8), which is the reception of 'power from on high' in order to be a witness to the Risen Lord and to participate in His ministry.

In v 2, there was a sound that came; it was "like" the rush of a mighty wind. The use of a single word with a dual reference to mean both "wind" and "spirit" was a shared phenomenon in

---

[13] Ibid., p.249.
[14] Ibid., p.321, n.2.

Hebrew, Aramaic and Greek. So the sound of the wind becomes an appropriate symbol to indicate the "blowing of the wind" or the coming of the Spirit. In a literal, physical sense there was no "mighty wind" that day, only a sound which pointed to a spiritual reality. The sound, although produced in the physical realm, was a divine manifestation, indicating the "Coming" of the long-awaited Holy Spirit, to inaugurate the age of the Spirit.

In v 3, there appeared a visual phenomenon; it was "like" a mass of fire, from which individual flames separated, moved to, and rested upon, each of the waiting believers. This being joined to Christ by the Spirit, when eschatologically understood, is the once-for-all constitution of the Church. But it also became a pattern for future converts. And this is what Paul calls being "baptized...by one Spirit...into one body" (1 Cor 12:13), and as such it is a repeatable event for others.

In v 4, we come to the climax: "They were all filled with the Holy Spirit." In vv 2 and 3, Luke had set forth signs which, at one and the same time, reported the empirical experience of the waiting Group and pointed beyond the signs to events of a vast, spiritual significance. Now he sets forth the invisible, inaudible event first, and then Proceeds to describe the sign which "began" to be manifested, viz., the speaking in "other tongues as the Spirit gave them utterance."

It seems to me that it can be safely argued that Luke understood the words "they were all filled with the Holy Spirit" (Ac 2:4) as fulfilling the various promises of Jesus which he (Luke) had just recorded, viz., (1) "you shall receive power when the Holy Spirit has come upon you" (Ac 1:8); (2) "before many days (i.e., in just a few days) you shall be baptized in the Holy Spirit" (Ac 1:5)[15]; and (3) "Behold, I send the promise of my

---

[15] *Baptize in*: All the passages in the New Testament that use a preposition following the word *baptize* use **en** (in), followed by a dative; those without a preposition are also followed by the dative. Both may be read as either instrumental (with) or locative (in). It is clear that proselyte baptism was

Father upon you; but tarry (or wait) in the city, until you are clothed with power from on high" (Lk 24:49).

The "speaking in tongues" is, in Paul's terms, a "manifestation of the Spirit." Luke, in describing this activity at Pentecost, simply says: "They were...filled...and began to speak." The grammatical subject of "began to speak" is both human and active. This is no divine ventriloquism, but a human-divine act of collaboration: "They spoke...as...the Spirit gave." It is as though two distinct streams of activity flow together and fuse into the one activity.

This requires, on the one hand, that the Spirit be active, but also, on the other hand, that the human side of the equation be active. If the Spirit is not active, i.e., if the Spirit is by-passed or excluded in any way, the activity that results is nothing but "the flesh," because it is done by the human self alone.

What does it mean that the human side of the equation be active? This has to include three levels of activity, and these can be described as: (1) a knowing-feeling (i.e., a discerning and an understanding of what the will of the Spirit is; (2) a willingness (i.e., a disposition and a decision); and (3) a doing-saying (i.e., the execution of the intent in word and/or act).

At the juncture where the human and the divine come together to produce the manifestation of the Spirit, Scripture sets forth three possible ways that the human side may act or react, viz., (1) humbly obey, (2) "grieve the Spirit", and (3) "quench the Spirit."[16]

Humble obedience should be normal for the believer. It is surely what God expects and what we, as spiritual believers, should understand. With Paul we understand that "humble"

---

total immersion and that John the Baptist followed the same practice ("We are seed of Abraham" is tantamount to saying, "We are not proselytes.") Because of the parallel between baptize in water and baptize in Spirit, I prefer the translation, "baptize **in** the Holy Spirit."

[16] See Chart No.1.

refers to our finitude, our fallibility, and our limitations; for "We know in part and we prophesy in part" (1 Cor 13:9).[17] To know and accept this makes for humility, makes submission one to another easier and works to undercut arrogance. It should also make us more desirous of knowing the mind of the Spirit and of being aware of any resistance in us to the divine will.

A second way that the human side may react is to "grieve the Holy Spirit" (Eph 4:30). This may be done at the three levels of knowing, willing and doing, by being insensitive, unwilling and disobedient. May the cry of our heart be: "Lord, make me sensitive; make me willing; make me obedient."

The third way of reacting to the Holy Spirit is to "quench the Spirit" (1 Th 5:20). This goes beyond and is more drastic than "to grieve." To quench is "to extinguish fire," to stifle, or to suppress. Paul seems to intimate that this can be done in two ways: (1) by despising (i.e., down-grading and undervaluing) the activity of the Holy Spirit and (2) by not "testing" (i.e., examining and proving) the "spiritual" activity in the congregation. The first of these says "no" to all activity of the Spirit; and the second says "yes" uncritically to everything that claims to be spiritual. Both of these attitudes will eventually put out the fires of the Holy Spirit in a congregation.

To conclude this section, let us look anew at the point of interaction between the human and the divine. The Holy Spirit knows what is in a person, even below the levels of what we recognize and know. He knows that we are flesh, weak, limited, mortal, fallible, etc. But still He respects our consciousness, our freedom, our integrity, and our dignity. He is both sensitive and willing to work with us. We, on our part, must

---

[17] RSV: "Our knowledge is imperfect and our prophecy is imperfect"; Phillips: "Our knowledge is always incomplete and our prophecy is always incomplete"; and NEB: "Our knowledge and our prophecy alike are partial."

respect and honor the Holy Spirit. We must be sensitive and obedient.[18]

III

Now, let us examine the ways in which these principles apply to, and are worked out in, the different spiritual gifts. The context of the spiritual gifts, in a general sense, is the church, the gathered people of God. During the wilderness period in the Old Testament, the LORD manifested his 'presence with His people' in the Pillar of Fire by night and the Pillar of Cloud by day, which stood over the tent of meeting in the midst of the camp. When Moses chose the seventy elders to assist him, "the LORD came down in the cloud and spoke to him, and took some of the Spirit that was upon him and put it upon the seventy elders; and when the Spirit rested upon them, they prophesied" (Nu 11:25). But two of the elders, who were back in the camp, also received the Spirit and prophesied. This was reported to Moses as though it were in some way a profaning of the Holy, and Moses replied, "Are you jealous for my sake? Would that all the LORD'S people were prophets, that the LORD would put his Spirit upon them!" (v 29).

Much later that prophetic hope was boldly announced by the mouth of the prophet Joel, "I will pour out my Spirit on all flesh; your sons and your daughters shall prophesy" (Joel 2:28). As we all know, this prophecy was fulfilled on the Day of Pentecost. But what we often forget is that now again, since Pentecost, a spiritual Pillar of Fire, viz., the presence of the Triune God, stands in the midst of His gathered people ("where two or three are gathered in my name, there am I in the midst of them" Mt 18:20), but with this difference: now each believer

---

[18] See Chart No.2. This recaps the possible sources of spiritual activity: (1) the demonic, which invades and short-circuits the human spirit; (2) the flesh, which is in operation when the human self generates "spiritual" activity and the Holy Spirit is short-circuited; and (3) the Biblical model, in which the Holy Spirit and the human spirit cooperate in mutual respect and sensitivity.

is linked to the Divine Presence by the Holy Spirit and can be used of the Spirit "as He wills" and as we are sensitive and obedient.

Both in 1 Cor 12:4-6 and in Eph 4:4-6 Paul speaks of the Spirit, the Lord and God, in that order, which corresponds to the fact that one's immediate contact is with the Spirit, and through the Spirit to Christ and through Christ to the Father.[19] From the one overriding fact of Christian existence, viz., that "through the Spirit" we are made to be "in Christ," we have the two fundamental principles governing all exercise of spiritual gifts and all performance of Christian ministry, viz., that all is done (1) in Christ and (2) through the power of the Holy Spirit.

Paul in his second letter to the Corinthians sets forth a principle of polarity which applies here (5:20). The Christian believer is both active and passive as he relates to the Divine.[20] One is both an ambassador (i.e., an active agent and a representative) and a vessel (i.e., a passive instrument and channel). As an ambassador one has been given authority, i.e., the delegated right to act in the name of his Lord ("we beseech you on behalf of Christ"). As a vessel one has received power ("God making His appeal through us").

What matters in authority is (1) that one be duly authorized and (2) that one properly use that authority. At the end of each of the Gospels there is a reference to Christ delegating authority to His disciples (and by inference, to subsequent generations of believers).

1. Matthew writes (28:18f): "All authority in heaven and on earth has been given to me. Go therefore and make disciples of all nations, baptizing them in the name of the Father and of the Son and the Holy Spirit."

---

[19] See Chart No.3.
[20] See Chart No.4.

2. Mark writes (16:17).: "And these signs shall follow them that believe: in my name they will cast out demons, etc. (i.e., do ministry)."
3. Luke writes (24:46-49): "Thus it is written, Messiah is to suffer and to rise from the dead on the third day, and in His name repentance and forgiveness of sins are to be preached unto all nations...You are witnesses...but wait...until you are clothed with power from on high."
4. John writes (20:21-23): "As the Father has sent me, even so send I you...Whosoever sins you forgive, they are forgiven."

Thus on the active side, the believer is given the right to use the authority of the name of his Lord. He is an agent who can act on behalf of Christ.

On the passive side, the believer is a vessel or a conductor of the power of God. That power is linked to the presence of the Holy Spirit. "You shall receive power, when the Holy Spirit has come upon you" (Ac 1:8). And that power is always of God; and the glory is always His. "We have this treasure in earthen vessels," says Paul, "to show that the transcendent power belongs to God and not to us" (2 Co 4:7). We are "**Bearers of the Presence**"; and our presence should serve to communicate the presence of the Holy One. Our touch and our word may serve to communicate the power and wisdom of God. Even tokens sent from the bodies of His servants may serve as channels of power (Ac 19:12).

IV

Finally, let us look at the Fruit of the Spirit and the Gifts of the Spirit. The Fruit of the Spirit is what the Spirit is endeavoring to do *in us*, viz., to conform us to the likeness of Jesus. The Gifts of the Spirit are what the Spirit is endeavoring to do *through us*. It is possible to be so preoccupied with either one of these that the other is neglected. Both are workings of the Spirit, and both are necessary.

In the first chapter of his first letter to the Corinthians, Paul discusses some categories which are useful not only for understanding the gospel, but also for interpreting spiritual gifts. He says that Christ sent him "to preach the gospel, not with eloquent wisdom, lest the cross of Christ be emptied of its power. For the word of the cross...is the power of God" (1 Cor 1:17f). And again, "We preach Christ crucified...Christ the power of God and the wisdom of God" (vv 23f).

Three of the concepts found here in chapter 1, viz., the Wisdom of God, the Power of God, and the Word of the Cross could very well serve as categories to organize the spiritual gifts which Paul lists in chap. 12. The spiritual gifts fall into three categories: (1) Gifts of Revelation (cf. the Wisdom of God, the Greeks sought wisdom); (2) Gifts of Power (cf. the Power of God, the Jews demanded signs, i.e., miracles); and (3) the Gifts of Communication (cf. the Word of the Cross, which both Jew and Gentile must hear).

The Two Gifts of Revelation

The two Gifts of Revelation are: (1) the Word of Wisdom and (2) the Word of Knowledge.

The WORD OF WISDOM is an insightful, new understanding, communicated by the Spirit, concerning (a) some aspect of spiritual truth or (b) some course to be followed either by the church or an individual. The apostles and elders in Acts 15 apparently felt that they had received a word of wisdom from the Spirit, when, in reference to the decision about receiving Gentiles into fellowship without circumcision (v 28), they said that "it seemed good to the Holy Spirit and to us."

The WORD OF KNOWLEDGE is a communication from the Spirit about some truth or fact heretofore unknown. Peter apparently received a word of knowledge when he received a communication from the Spirit that a certain property was not sold for a stated price.

The two gifts of revelation seem to function in the following way: (1) the Spirit insinuates a thought into the believer's mind (e.g., "this is how this is to be understood," or "this is what is to be done," or "this is how it is."), and (2) the Spirit causes the spirit of the believer to know that this is from Him and not from another.

In cases of revelation, spiritual sensitivity and discernment are especially important. The message to the churches in Asia is not amiss here: "He who has an ear, let him hear what the Spirit is saying to the church" (Rev 2:7, 11, 17, 27; 3:6, 13, 22).

The Three Gifts of Power

The three Gifts of Power are (1) faith, (2) gifts of healing, and (3) working of miracles.[21]

The GIFT OF FAITH is not saving faith, nor the faith by which we walk, but a special faith given by the Spirit to accomplish the otherwise impossible. Paul apparently associated this faith (1 Cor 13:2) with the teaching of Jesus on the "faith that moves mountains" (Mt 17:20; 21:21f; Mark 11:22f; Luke 17:6). This faith comes with a feeling of power and the full assurance that it will be done; it is spoken forth in words that would appear reckless in an ordinary situation. The word of faith has a certain "name-it-and-claim-it" ring. But there is a difference; it is the Spirit, with the sensitive obedience of the Christian, who names what shall be done and thus so recklessly announces it. Such seems to have been Paul's word to Elymas (Acts 13:8-11).

The GIFTS OF HEALING (*healing* is plural in the Greek) work parallel to natural healing, which, although taken for granted, is

---

[21] *Healing* and *working* are both plural in the Greek

not generally understood. Divine healing is like a speeding-up of the natural healing process, and involves the imparting of healing power, which comes from God, either directly or through His servant.[22] If touch is involved, the flow of healing power may at times be felt (cf. Mark 5:30). In personal ministry, I have found it helpful (1) to endeavor to be a channel of God's love and compassion, (2) to pray in Christ's name and according to His promise and provision, and (3) to ask that this be done for God's glory alone.

There is a depth of mystery to healings. We often say, when someone is not healed, that we do not understand why. The truth, of course, is that we do not understand either why or how, when God *does* heal.

The <u>WORKING OF MIRACLES</u> (*working* is plural in the Greek) involves the interposition of Divine power to accomplish what would, otherwise, either not be done or be impossible. The making of the paralytic walk at the Beautiful Gate is a splendid example. There was a revelation to God's ministers of His intent to work a special miracle in this case. They were sensitive and obedient; but it was the power of God that wrought the miracle.

As the gifts of revelation draw on the wisdom of God in Christ, so the gifts of power draw on the power of God in Christ. The servant of the Lord becomes the channel for that power to flow through, in order to accomplish that purpose for which the Lord sends it forth.

The Gifts of Communication

Third, for our consideration, in Paul's list of spiritual gifts are two pairs of gifts of communication. Each pair has a primary gift and complementary gift. These are, respectively, (1) the

---

[22] We are correct when we speak of "divine healing" and not "faith healing." There are many faith healers who are neither Christian nor religious.

gift of prophecy with the gift of discerning of spirits and (2) the gift of tongues with the gift of interpretation of tongues.

PROPHECY AND THE DISCERNING OF SPIRITS

PROPHECY is a speaking forth (or forth-telling) of some message from God to others for their edification, exhortation, or comfort, and in the case of foretelling, for their instruction and action. Paul reminded us that "we prophesy in part" (1 Cor 13:9), i.e., that we receive and transmit somewhat less than all of what the Spirit is communicating. It is very important to understand this.

Prophecy happens, at times, when a person is speaking to the church and by the Spirit is lifted to another level. Prophecy, on occasion, can function on the basis of being given word-for-word by the Spirit, but more commonly functions as the communication of intentionality and concepts (i.e., whole thoughts). The purity of Prophecy would then depend on the spiritual sensitivity of the speaker.

DISCERNING OF SPIRITS should function alongside of the Gift of Prophecy, because it is important that we be certain that the communication is From the Lord. Paul said, "Let the others judge (discern)," i.e., let them ascertain the spiritual source from which the inspiration comes (14:29). There are three possibilities: the Holy Spirit, the flesh, and the demonic. Discerning of spirits is equally related to, and is often classified with, the gifts of revelation. It consists of an inner witness, either confirming or disavowing the message which is going forth.

KINDS OF TONGUES AND INTERPRETATION

Kinds of tongues and interpretation of tongues form the second pair of gifts of communication.

TONGUES is the speaking forth of a verbal communication in a language or tongue unknown to the speaker. This has been treated above. The gift that complements tongues for public use is the gift of interpretation of tongues.

INTERPRETATION OF TONGUES is not just a translation, but a speaking forth, in one's own or a known language, of the "sense" or "meaning" of a tongue, as that meaning or "interpretation" is captured from the Spirit. As far as the transmission process goes, it functions almost identically to that of prophecy.

In brief summary: in this paper we have explored the interaction of the Holy Spirit and the human spirit in the operation of spiritual gifts. We have discovered that the demonic negates and invades, while the Holy Spirit woos, invites, and gives, but then waits for us to receive and obey.

I close with two remarks: first, the Holy Spirit is active, both in us as individuals and in us as a church, molding and making each of us more and more into the image of God's dear Son, but we must be pliable and amenable to His working. And second, He is also active in continuing the ministry of Christ through us and wishes to use us even beyond our natural abilities in communicating the wisdom, the power and the word of God to others.

We are living in a time of great hunger for spiritual reality, and this is partly due to the failings of Christians in past generations to be occupied with spiritual things. Today the floodgates of darkness (the demonic and the occult) are filling the void. It behooves us as Pentecostals to perpetuate and disseminate the spiritual heritage which we have received.

Charts

Chart No. 1
Possible Reactions to the Holy Spirit
(Footnote 16)

Activity ➤	Cooperate	Grieve	Quench
Passage ➤	1 Cor 13:9	Eph 4:30	1 Th 5:19
Knowing	'in part'	insensitive	No!
Willing	willing	unwilling	No!
Saying-Doing	'in part'	disobedient	No!

Chart No. 2
Kinds of Spiritual Manifestations
(Footnote 18)

1. Demonic Possession

The Human   The Demonic

Demonic Possession

When the demonic spirit over-rides the human spirit, there is demon possession.

2. Operating in the Flesh

The Human   The Divine

Operating in the Flesh

When the human spirit acts without the Holy Spirit, the flesh is acting.

3. Operating in the Spirit

The Human   The Divine

Operating in the Spirit

When the Holy Spirit gives and the human spirit obeys, the gifts of the Spirit operate.

Chart No. 3
The Context of Spiritual Gifts
(Footnote 19)

		God		
	Love		Love	
	|		|	
Wisdom	|	Word	|	Power
	|		|	
	|	Holy Spirit	|	
	|		|	
		The Church		
	↘		↘	
	Fruit	of the	Spirit	
The Fruit of the Spirit: God's Work in us.				
	Gifts	of the	Spirit	
The Gifts of the Spirit: God's Work Through us.				
Gifts of Revelation		Gifts of Communication		Gifts of Power

Chart No. 4
The Nature of Ministry - 2 Cor 5:20
(Footnote 20)

Active	Passive
We beseech you in the name of Christ	God makes his appeal Through us
Authority = in the name of Jesus Christ	**Power =** Through the Holy Spirit
I give you authority delegation of authority responsible use	You shall receive power fullness of the Spirit compassionate touch & word
Ambassador = agent-representative right to use the authority	**Vessel =** instrument-channel privilege - channel of power

A Wedding Song

Father, we gather to praise you,
Your spirit unites us as one;
Be present and bless now this wedding,
Joining the two in your love.

Refrain:
In your own image you made us,
With love that engenders new life;
Come now in your grace; bless this union,
Making them husband and wife.

Lord, at the wedding in Cana,
You gave them a wonderful sign;
Come now in your grace, touch the water,
Change it again into wine

Here is the bride; here is the groom;
We ask, Lord, that this may be done;
Unite them this day by your power,
Making the two of them one.

Written in Cleveland in the 1990s. Note: the rhythm in the third verse changes.

PROPHECY
Linguistic Considerations

Etymology: The English verb *prophesy* is a transliteration from the Greek (πρόφημι = pró-fay-me), and the Greek word is a compound word, composed of 'pro' (πρό) meaning *before* or *forth* and 'phemi' (φημί), meaning *to say, speak* or *utter*.

Word Cluster: There are several other words in this word cluster, built on the verb *prophesy* (προφητεύω = pró-fay-téw-oh):

1. the masculine and feminine forms of the noun, indicating the person who does the prophesying: prophet (προφήτης = pro-fáy-tace) and prophetess (προφῆτις = pro-fáy-tees),[1]
2. the noun form which indicates the message or what was spoken: prophecy (προφητεία = pro-fay- táy-ah), and
3. the adjective meaning "of the prophets" or describing that which has the property or character of prophecy: prophetical (προφητικός = pro-fay-tee-kós).[2]

---

[1] The feminine form is used only two times in the New Testament, once of Anna (Lk 2:36) and once of Jezebel of Thyatira, who is said to have called herself a prophetess (Rev 2:20). However Luke records that Philip had four unmarried daughters who prophesied (Ac 21:9).

[2] This form is used twice in the New Testament: once by Paul (Rom 16:26) referring to the prophetic writings (the scriptures) which give witness to the mystery of Christ, and once by Peter (2 Pe 1:19-21), referring the gospel message as the prophetic word (KJ: a...word of prophecy).

Theological

The function of prophecy: The function of prophecy in the
New Testament must be understood by the basic definition of
that function in the Old Testament, viz., the true prophet was
the one who had a true word from God for the people. In fact,
Moses spoke words that correctly describe the prophetic function in the New Testament: "Would that all the Lord's people
were prophets, that the Lord would put his Spirit upon them"
(Nu 11:29). This happened at Pentecost, where the Spirit
came, the church was constituted and the believers, including
the converts, were baptized in the Holy Spirit. Under the new
covenant the Spirit is for all, Jew and Gentile, slave and free,
male and female. Peter quoted Joel as saying that the Spirit
would be poured out on all flesh and that both sons and daughters would prophesy. Mainline Protestants give importance, as
we do, to the priesthood of all believers, but we as Pentecostals
must also emphasize the Prophethood of all believers: we are
all speakers for the Lord, even the new convert; for Jesus told
the Gadarene, "Go home to your friends and tell them what
great things the Lord has done for you and has had compassion
on you" (Mk 5:19).

The popular understanding of prophecy is too much influenced by the idea of foretelling, although foretelling may be a
part of prophecy. I see the Old Testament prophets as basically
fulfilling the purposes of prophecy as set forth by Paul, viz.,
edification, exhortation and comfort (1 Cor 14:3), and then, in
connection with these, foretelling certain things.. When God's
people are weak they need building up, when they fall behind
or go astray they need exhortation to turn back to the Lord and
go on, and when they suffer they need comfort. God's promises and warnings for the future generally came and still come
in these contexts.

Prophecy and Discernment: In Paul's listing of the spiritual
gifts in his first letter to the Corinthians, prophecy and discernment are linked together as a pair just before the final pair

of tongues and interpretation (1 Cor 12:10; 14:29; see also 1 Th 5:19-21). John also in his first epistle speaks of trying the spirits (4:1-3). The important matter in receiving prophecy is to know if it comes from the Lord or not. It may be of the flesh, i.e., of human origin.

Questions

Is prophecy for individual guidance?

❖ Not primarily so. A word of prophecy should never be taken as the only basis for an individual to act, but may be a confirmation of what the Lord has already said to one. Prophecies came forth at the ordination of Timothy and he received a charisma (gift) at the same time (1 Tim 1:18, 4:14). The two prophecies of Agabus in Acts are in the nature of forewarning, so that those involved could prepare, although Paul's friends wanted to draw other conclusions from the second prophecy.

Does giving a word of prophecy make one a prophet?

❖ Not necessarily so. There were those who were called prophets in the early church, but Peter said that the fullness of the Spirit was for all flesh and Paul said that "all of you can prophesy one by one." In Acts the title of prophet/s is given three times (1) to a group from Jerusalem, that visited in Antioch, the only one of which is named is Agabus, (11:27; 21:10), (2) to the pastoral staff at Antioch, the five are called "prophets and teachers" (13:1), and (3) to Judas and Silas, the two delegates from Jerusalem who were appointed, after the so-called Jerusalem Conference, to visit the gentile churches in and around Antioch (15:27,32). Paul recognizes prophets as one of the gifts of Christ to his church (Eph. 4:11) but also maintains the prophetic nature of the whole body of the Church, and even uses the term *prophet* of any member when that person uses the gift of prophecy (1 Cor 12:28, 14:29, 32, 37). I would call Paul a writing prophet of the new Covenant.

Does a word of prophecy have the authority of Scripture?

❖   I say no, because as Paul said, "We know in part and we prophesy in part" (1 Cor 13:9). The person giving this particular prophecy may not have captured one hundred percent of what the Spirit is saying to the church. But even if the prophecy is exactly what the Spirit was saying, we are to understand that this was directed to a specific congregation, and not meant for others half-way around the world.

Is a prophecy, from a local context, of universal validity?

❖   The answer is no. God caused to be written down and brought together what he wants to share with the church in all times and places. Even then, the first situation spoken to was that of the first century, whether at Thessalonica, Philippi or Corinth.

Conclusion

Prophecy then is an inspired, charismatic message or word, given by the Spirit, through a believer in the common language of both the speaker and the hearer. Its purpose is edification, motivation or comfort and may include an announcement of future events for the purpose of either warning or inspiring hope. All prophecy is subject to discernment and we should be humble enough to admit, in any particular context, that perhaps we did not capture the full meaning of what the Spirit is saying to the Church.

Part Two

The Christian Life

ॐ ✿ ॐ

THE POWER OF CONSECRATION [*]

God has chosen the weak things of the world
to confound the mighty.
1 Cor 1:27

P aul wrote these words to the church in Corinth: "Consider this, my brothers and sisters, that among you who were called, there were not many wise according to the flesh, nor many mighty, nor many born into nobility. But God has chosen the foolish things of the world to confound the wise; he has chosen the weak things of the world to confound the mighty" (1 Cor 1:26-27).

W hen we, as Christians, consider who we are and what we possess in this world, we are sometimes tempted to be discouraged because we feel too small to do anything for God. We think that the little we have to offer him will be of no value to him. To think this way is praiseworthy, provided we do not forget that when what we are and what we have is consecrated to the Lord, he is able, with that little bit, to do great things. Yes, the Lord is able to use weak things to confound the mighty.

O ne day Jesus lifted up his eyes and saw the rich people putting their offerings into the treasury of the temple. He also saw a poor widow, as she was putting two small pieces of money into the treasury, and he said to his disciples, "To tell the truth, this poor widow has given more than all the rest, because they

---

[*] This article was written and published in French as an editorial in
L'Evangile, the official organ of the Church of God in Haiti, in its issue of
March-April, 1953, pp. 2-5. It was translated into English by the author.

gave of their surplus, but she has given, out of her poverty, all
that she had to live on" (Lk 21:14).   Why does the Lord praise
this poor widow?   And why did the offering of this poor, unfortunate woman have more value in his eyes than that of the
rest?

In the first place, it was because this offering was presented to
God and to Him alone, contrary to the offerings of the Phari-
sees, who gave to be seen of men.   The widow knew how little
her offering was in the sight of men, but still that did not hinder
her from presenting it to God.   She gave what little she had,
because she was not giving it to men, nor for the approval of
men.   But she still gave it because she was giving it to God and
to him alone.

In the second place, she gave out of what she needed.   Jesus
remarked that the others gave out of their surplus; that is, they
gave from what they did not need for themselves.   But the
widow gave all that she had to live on.   We should compare
our offering to that of this widow.   First, do we sincerely offer
our offering to God and to God alone?   Or do we sometimes
give to be seen of men?   Or, on the other hand, do we refuse to
give because we do not like our pastor's way of doing things?
And second, do we give out of what we need or out of our surplus?   Do we faithfully pay our tithes, or do we only pay tithes
when we have received a little more money that we regularly
do?   And finally, do we make a real sacrifice when we present
our offering to God?

This story about the widow also teaches us that God not only
takes note of the offering, but also of the one who offers.   The
Master of Heaven and Earth is not poor, that he should be enriched by the offerings of anyone.   He prefers to receive a
humble offering accompanied with the heart of the giver, rather
than a royal offering--no matter how royal it may be--that is
not accompanied with the heart of the giver.   The material and
visible offering should be the symbol of the gift of ourselves.

There is no gift that can replace the gift of ourselves and of our hearts to God.

Let us also remember that God does not appreciate an offering in proportion to its grandeur or its material value. And neither is God limited by its small value. One time Jesus fed a whole multitude (about four thousand men, without counting the women and children) with only seven pieces of bread and some fish (Mt 15:30f). One humble offering, sincerely given to God, can become the means of a great blessing for a whole multitude. And the Old Testament teaches us that a little girl from the country of Israel told Naaman, the head of the Syrian army, that, in Israel, there was a prophet who could heal him. By means of the simple testimony of that humble servant, Naaman was healed of his leprosy.

You also may be little in this world, but if your life is consecrated to the service of the Master, it will become, by the Holy Spirit, a source of blessing for those around you. That which is weak, if consecrated to the Lord, becomes strong in his almighty hands.

Sometimes when I am praying for the churches and thinking of the needs of our work in Haiti, I have asked myself, "What would the Church of God become and what would it be able to accomplish if all of its members would sincerely consecrate themselves and their talents, however small, to the service of the Lord?" I am sure that we would see great things happen. Below I have listed five things that I desire with all my heart for every member of the Church of God in Haiti; and I am persuaded that if each member would do these five things, we would soon see revival break out in our midst.

1. That each member be completely consecrated to God.
   ❖ This means that each member would be sanctified and baptized in the Holy Spirit and fire.

2. That each member diligently study the Word of God.
   * ❖ This means that each member would walk in submission to the Word of God.
3. That each member would intercede for those who are lost, and for the advancement of the Kingdom of God in Haiti.
   * ❖ This means that each member would have a burden for the salvation of souls and a desire for the Work of God to advance.
4. That each member would testify and tell others what Christ has done for him or her.
   * ❖ This means that each member would become an ambassador for Christ and would lead others to the Lord.
5. That each member would faithfully pay his or her tithes.
   * ❖ This means that each member would support the Work with his or her money.

Paul, in his letter to the Romans, exhorted them in these terms, "I beseech you therefore, brethren, by the mercies of God, that ye present your bodies a living sacrifice, holy, acceptable unto God, which is your reasonable service" (Rom 12:1). God asks of us a complete consecration, and it is reasonable that we submit ourselves to Him who redeemed us and gave us eternal life. My brothers and sisters, consecrate yourselves, your body, your time, your activities, your talents and your money completely to God, and He will bless you and make you a blessing. For victory, true victory, is only found in complete consecration.

ॐ ✿ ☙

THE NATURE AND RESULTS
OF THANKFULNESS [1]

What is thankfulness? Did you ever stop to think about it? To hear people talk---and even at that they don't talk about thankfulness very much--you would think that it is only part of being a good, moral person, or part of being a courteous and cultured person, or part of being a loyal and patriotic citizen. We hear very little preaching on the "grace" of thankfulness, but both the Old and the New Testaments are full of it.

If you turn to the dictionary for a definition of *thankful* and *thankfulness*, you will find meanings such as these: grateful; "appreciative of benefits received;"[2] and acknowledgment for a favor or kindness received. For *appreciate* you will find definitions such as: (1) to set a just value on, or to esteem the full worth of, something ; (2) to approve of, or to be grateful for, something; (3) to be sensitive to the aesthetic values of, or to be cognizant of, something.[3]

Based on this, I think we can say that thankfulness, in the sense of being thankful to God, is the appreciative response of the receiving heart to God's grace and unmerited favor. We have examples of this in Scripture: (1) the woman who washed Jesus' feet; (2) the palsied man "borne of four" and let down through the housetop (Lk 5:25); (3) the woman "which had a spirit of infirmity eighteen years" (Lk 13:13); (4) the Samaritan leper, one of the ten whom Jesus healed (Lk 17:15f);

---

[1] This article was published twice in the *Church of God Evangel*, 54:38 (Nov 23, 1964), p. 12 and 58:37 (Nov 25, 1968), p. 12.
[2] *Webster's Seventh New Collegiate Dictionary* (Springfield: G. & C. Merriam Company, 1966), p. 914.
[3] *Ibid.* p. 43.

(5) the blind beggar of Jericho (Luke 18:43); and (6) the lame man by the Beautiful gate (Ac 3:8). The expressions of thankfulness by these and many others are in such words as "glorify, give thanks, praise, magnify, and bless." Thus we see that when God's gracious blessings are received, the receiving heart responds, or at least should respond, in appreciation and thankfulness.

The word *thankfulness* is dependent on prepositions. We are thankful *to* someone *for* something, whether to a friend for a favor, or to God for His blessings. The biblical exhortations to thankfulness urge us to be thankful to God, the Giver of every good and perfect gift (Jas 1:17), through his Son, Jesus Christ. "Give thanks to God and the Father by him" (Col 3:17). And the *for* of thankfulness! When we "count (y)our many blessings (and) see what God has done,"[4] we should not only think of the material blessings of life, as so many are prone to do, but we should also remember our spiritual blessings. It is wonderful that God has given us health and strength and happiness, a sound mind, a good home, friends who are kind, freedom, liberty, and an innumerable list of other things. The Christian recognizes that one can possess all these things, yet without the spiritual blessings of God, he will be "wretched, and miserable, and poor, and blind, and naked" (Rev 3:17). Whoever has received the grace of God into one's heart and life can exclaim with Paul:

> Blessed be the God and Father of our Lord Jesus Christ, who has blessed us with all spiritual blessings in heavenly places in Christ. In whom we have redemption through his blood, the forgiveness of sins, according to the riches of his grace. ... In whom also we have obtained an inheritance. ... In whom we have boldness and access with confidence by the faith of him (Eph 1:3,7,11; 3:12). Thanks be to God for his unspeakable gift (2 Cor 9:15).

---

[4] From the gospel song, "Count Your Blessings" by Johnson Oatman, Jr.

Now what is the cause or basis of thankfulness? It is not altogether in God's blessings because there are many who receive of His blessings who are not thankful. It is the "glad and free recognition of our indebtedness to God"[5] The Patriarch Jacob knew this truth: "I am not worthy, in the least, of all the acts of mercy and faithfulness that you have shown your servant; for with my staff I passed over this Jordan; and now I am become two bands" (Gen 32:10).

David, the man after God's own heart, also knew. After the people had brought generous offerings for the construction of the projected temple, he prayed:

> Blessed art thou, Lord God of Israel our father, for ever and ever. Thine, O Lord, is the greatness, and the power, and the glory, and the victory, and the majesty: for all that is in heaven and in earth is thine; thine is the kingdom, O Lord, and thou are exalted as head above all. Both riches and honour come of thee, and thou reignest over all; and in thine hand is power and might; and in thine hand it is to make great; and to give strength unto all. Now therefore, our God, we thank thee, and praise thy glorious name. But who am I, and what is my people, that we should be able to offer so willingly after this sort? for all things come of thee, and of thine own have we given thee (1 Chr 29:10-14).

Paul also saw the heart of the matter when he wrote to the Corinthians: "For who makes you to be different from anyone else? and what do you have that you did not receive? now if you received it, why do you glory, as if you had not received it?" (1 Cor 4:7). Is it life, a strong body, a sound mind, education, forgiveness of sins? Make the list as long as you can. Is there anything that you have not received, either directly or indirectly? How thankful we ought to be!

---

[5] C. E. B. Cranfield, "Thank" in Alan Richardson, ed., *A Theological Word Book of the Bible* (New York: MacMillan, 1951) p. 254.

Often, a consideration of the opposite of your subject will give you light on the subject at hand. Let us look for a moment at the nature of unthankfulness. Paul writes to Timothy,

> This know also, that in the last days perilous times shall come. For men shall be lovers of their own selves, covetous, boasters, proud, blasphemers, disobedient to parents, unthankful, unholy" (2 Tim 3:1f).

That is a résumé of the elements, characteristics, and companions of unthankfulness. It is the nature of unthankfulness to be selfish, grabbing for self, boasting of self, enthroning self, refusing to recognize any dependence or need. Selfishness is one of the gods of this world. "Little children, keep yourselves from idols" (1 Jn 5:21).[6]

The Results of Thankfulness

True thankfulness will always result in thanksgiving, and no thanksgiving will be true thanksgiving unless it is accompanied by true thankfulness in the heart. Thankfulness is the emotion or feeling of thanks, and thanksgiving is the action of expressing that thankfulness. Paul wrote to the Colossians: "Be thankful" (Col 3:15), and immediately in verse 17 he said, "... giving thanks to God and the Father by him." We should be thankful and give thanks; they are both part of Christian living.

For most persons, thanksgiving concerns the past. It should, however, concern past, present, and future--the blessings we received yesterday, the ones we are receiving today, and the ones He has promised for tomorrow. True thankfulness will give us gratitude for the past, joy for the present, and hope for the future.

Gratitude is closely allied to love. After Jesus had told Simon the Pharisee the parable of the creditor who forgave two debtors, He asked him, "Which of them will love him most?" He might have said, "Which of them will be more grateful?" Nei-

---

[6] See also Rom 1:18-32.

ther debtor would have loved him if he had not been grateful. Thus gratitude is an appreciative response to a favor received, and this, in turn, issues in love, the motive that prompted the blessing. As John said, "We love him, because he first loved us" (1 Jn 4:19). The order is: He loved us; He blessed us; we received His blessing; we were grateful for His blessing; we love Him.

There's nothing that gives joy like thanking God for His blessings. In fact, it seems to me that joy and thanks are inter-related in such a way that each produces the other in the hearts of God's children. Twice in his Epistles Paul mentions the bubbling up of that inward joy which issues in hymns and psalms and spiritual songs and making melody in our hearts. Both of these passages are followed by "giving thanks" in the very next verse: "Making melody in your heart ...giving thanks" (Eph 5:19f); "Singing with grace in your hearts ...giving thanks" (Col 3:16f). Most of our singing is an ex-pression of our joy and our thanks; so are many of the psalms.

Hope for the future. The future is for those who love God and who, by faith, can claim His promises and thank Him in ad-vance. "Hope that is seen is not hope" (Rom 8:24). Can we claim His promises without thanking Him? I doubt it. As Je-sus stood outside the open tomb of Lazarus, He lifted His eyes toward heaven and said, "Father, I thank you...." That was be-fore one thing happened. Why did He thank Him? "I thank you because you have heard me. And I knew that you always hear me..." (Jn 11:41f). He thanked Him because He knew He could depend on Him. His promises are sure, but are we sure of His promises? If we are, we can thank Him and have hope for the future, as Cransfield says,

> Thankfulness, the glad and free recognition of our infinite indebtedness to God, is the one true motive of Christian liv-ing; cf. Mt 10:8; 18:32; 1 Cor 6:20; Eph 4:32. The same

idea is behind Mt 25:31; for our gratitude to Christ is to be rendered to the neighbor who comes as his representative.[7]

As Paul puts it, "Whatsoever you do in word or deed, do all in the name of the Lord Jesus, giving thanks to God and the Father by him" (Col 3:17).

Now let us consider the practical results of thankfulness in word and deed, first in our relationship with God, then in our relationship with others.

In the epistle to the Hebrews (13:15f) we have compacted in two verses what should be the expression of our thankfulness toward God in word and deed. It is put very beautifully in terms of an altar and sacrifice, for truly we do have an altar (13:10). Our sacrifice is not for sin, however, for the prophet Micah said, "Will the Lord be pleased with thousands of rams, or with ten thousands of rivers of oil? Shall I give my firstborn for my transgressions, the fruit of my body for the sin of my soul?" (6:7). No, "For it is not possible that the blood of bulls and of goats should take away sins" (Heb 10:4). "Wherefore Jesus also, that he might sanctify the people with his own blood, suffered without the gate" (13:12). Jesus, the Lamb of God who takes away the sin of the world, offered Himself as our sin offering. Nothing else would suffice. Our offering is a thank offering.

Let us, then, go forth to him outside the camp, bearing his reproach... (and) by him let us offer our sacrifice of praise to God, that is, the fruit of our lips, giving thanks to his name" (Heb 13:13,15). We like to think of "the throne of grace" where we can go to "obtain mercy, and find grace to help in time of need" (Heb 4:16). But after that we should not forget to offer our "sacrifice of praise," i.e., "the fruit of our lips giving thanks to his name." Heaven's portals are thronged with those who say, "Give me, Lord; I need your help." But few there be who take the time to come into his presence and give

---

[7] Cranfield, "Thank" p. 254.

him "Thanks". How often He has said, "Were there not ten cleansed? Where are the nine?" Let us remember to praise Him "continually."

Besides our sacrifice of praise, i.e., words from a thankful heart, what else is included in our sacrifice to God? Besides our sacrifice of words, Hebrews (13:16) continues by speaking of actions or deeds: "But to do good and to communicate (that means to give) forget not: for with such sacrifices God is well pleased." We can summarize these two actions in two phrases: good living and good giving.

Paul, likewise, exhorts the Romans to "present your bodies (as) a living sacrifice...unto God" (12:1). All that we are, say and do should be offered continually to God for his glory and as a means for God's grace and glory to touch others.

Thus Scripture teaches us to be thankful in our innermost being and to express that thankfulness in praise, living for God's glory and sacrificial giving.
For none of us lives for himself,
and no one dies for himself.
For if we live, we live for the Lord;
and if we die, we die for the Lord:
so whether we live, or whether we die,
we belong to the Lord. (Rom 14:7f)

Yes, both what we do and how we live, along with our praise to God, is a sweet smelling savor to Him. Our praise, our living and our giving, whether tithes, offerings or alms, is primarily "to the Lord." Both living and giving are sacrifices well pleasing unto Him. ✢

The Lord's Prayer

ෂ)ෑ

Our Father in heaven,
May your Name be honored as holy,
May your Kingdom come
And your Will be done,
On earth as it is in heaven!

Give us this day the bread that we need,
And forgive us where we have failed you,
As we have forgiven those who have failed us,

And lead us not into temptation,
But deliver us from evil.

For the Kingdom, and the Power, and the Glory
Are yours for ever and ever!

Amen!

Hallelujah!

ENTIRE SANCTIFICATION
By Leonard W. Sisk [1]
A Digest by James M. Beaty [2]

Preface for the Second Printing
by Vessie D. Hargrave

L.W. Sisk was a scholarly teacher who left indelible impressions on his students and fellow faculty members. His contributions to foreign missions may best be determined by the success of those whom he taught, particularly at the International Preparatory Institute.

Men and women who sat under this saintly man as he so capably taught in his classroom are now filling places of supervisory and educational leadership in the World Missions program of the Church of God.

---

[1] Lone Washington Sisk (name used in applications for credentials), was born October 23, 1895. In 1935, when he was licensed as an Evangelist in Rome, Georgia (No. 4181) on December 6, 1935, he had just joined the Church of God. He was a college graduate, had been preaching for twelve years and had been an ordained Itinerant in the Methodist Episcopal Church South. His first wife had died and he was married to a woman whose first husband had died. He was ordained in San Antonio, Texas on February 8, 1951, when he was fifty-five years old. There had been some kind of hiatus in his ministry, apparently because his second wife had divorced him and he had surrendered his first credentials. At the time of his ordination his second wife was deceased.   For some years before he died he taught at International Preparatory Institute.. He died on or about July 13, 1952, soon after he was ordained. This little book was published by the author with no indication of place and date. A second edition was printed by International Preparatory Institute, after his death.

[2] Athough the editor does not agree with Sisk on every point, he considers it of vital importance that we still hear and wrestle with these dimensions of faith and practice. Summaries and comments by the editor are in italics.

Entire Sanctification represents the firm convictions of the author relative to a life of holiness. This second edition of his work is provided to fill a need in the spiritual life of Christians for "such a time as this." My friend and colleague answered the "roll call" while on the teaching staff of I.P.I.

Vessie D. Hargrave
President 1946-1953

Introduction

As a doctrine and as an experience of divine grace, entire sanctification is the most hated and persistently rejected of all the principles presented to us in the Holy Scriptures.

In the following pages I shall endeavor to prove that Entire Sanctification in Christian experience is a second and an instantaneous work of divine grace, obtainable by faith on the part of the fully justified believer.

As a proper approach to the above proposition, it is necessary for me to discuss sin, of which the two works of grace have to do. There are two works of grace necessary in the full salvation of the human soul because sin is twofold in its nature. First, the transgression of the Law of God; second, the state of pollution and depravity which exists in the human nature.

Chapter One
Natural Depravity

Every child of Adam's race is totally depraved from birth... man is a sinner by nature. The heart of mankind is so deceitful that it very often hides itself from itself, so that only the Holy Ghost can reveal its real condition.

The depraved human heart...is the fountainhead out of which flows all the issues of life. This is not an acquired condition, but an inherited corruption... A condition that is acquired by personal indulgence can be corrected by human skill and power, but an inherited moral state cannot be removed or corrected by any human process or power. Such a correction can be made only by the operation of the Holy Ghost and the means provided in the plan of redemption.*He cites Psalm 51:3 and Job 14:4*

Romans 7:17, "Now then, it is no more I that do it, but sin that dwelleth in me."

Here the apostle refers to the sin that dwelleth within, not sins recorded in heaven! It is well to note the difference in recorded sins and sin that is in the nature. One cannot repent of indwelling sin. It is imposed. We are not guilty of it, but we are cursed by it. It is not recorded against us, but it dwells with us. It is not an act. But a state.   *He cites Rom 6:20.*

...(N)atural depravity, or inherited sin, necessitates a work of grace dealing directly with such a state of corruption. Sanctification is that work of divine grace which deals the deathblow to that state of moral corruption which does so easily beset us.

Chapter Two
Sanctification and Its Accepted Definitions

I have given considerable attention to inward corruption or natural depravity because of its relations to the...doctrine of "Entire Sanctification." When we use the word "entire," we have no reference to maturity, but we mean entirely cleansed or washed from all sin and its pollution. We believe in progress and growth, but growth in grace is not sanctification.
He cites definitions from the following dictionaries: Webster, Century, Imperial, Worcester, and Standard, plus American Encyclopedia, which show that there is an "accepted" definition of sanctification as cleansing and as following justification.[3]

---

[3] One should not use the dictionary to theologize, but Sisk, it seems to me,

Chapter Three
**Accepted Definitions of
Sanctification by Theologians**

He cites Adam Clarke's commentary on Jn 17:17, which emphasizes both "to separate" and "to make holy or pure."

Methodist Episcopal Catechism:

"The act of divine grace whereby we are made holy...Not an experience to be reached by growth, but by an 'act of divine grace.'"

The Westminster Confession of Faith:

This shows that sanctification follows calling and regeneration, but not as a specific experience.

John Wesley:

Sanctification, in the proper sense, is an instantaneous deliverance from all sin and includes an instantaneous power then given always to cleave to God.

Pope's Theology (Vol. 1, p. 64):

Sanctification in its beginnings, process, and final issues is the full eradication of sin itself, which, reigning in the unregenerate, coexists with the new life in the regenerate, is abolished in the wholly sanctified.

Matthew Henry's Commentary: *He cites this.*

Samuel Rutherford:

This Scottish divine said,

> Christ is more to be loved for giving us sanctification than justification. It is in some respects greater love in Him to sanctify than to justify, for He maketh us like Himself in His own essential portraiture and image in sanctification.

---

is attempting to clarify terms and words, which is both proper and necessary.

Chapter Four
The New Birth vs Sanctification
as Separate Works of Grace

Since sin is two-fold in its nature; namely, sin (*as*) a principle of evil within the depraved nature of man, and sin (*as*) an outward act of disobedience or transgression of the law of God, it takes two works of divine grace to completely settle the sin question.

The works of grace dealing with sin are both instantaneous. Justification is a judicial act and is just as instantaneous as it is to sign a legal paper…. (Being) from above…is a sudden, instantaneous impartation of divine life to the soul which was dead in trespasses and in sin. The new birth is not eradication, but impartation.

The first things the devil did to Adam and Eve was to plant the desire in their hearts to disobey God. The desire to disobey is one thing and the act of disobeying is another. The sins which we have committed are recorded against us in heaven. The "sin principle" which was imposed upon us is deep in our human nature and cannot be forgiven, but it can be eradicated.

Chapter Five
Instantaneous Sanctification

Guilt is to be forgiven as a judicial act; defilement is to be cleansed as a priestly function. Christ is our high priest; "He suffered without the gate that He might sanctify the people with His own blood" (Heb. 13:12).

Paul was commissioned to preach sanctification by faith and not by growth, nor works (Ac 26:16,18):

> Rise, and stand upon thy feet: for I have appeared unto thee for this purpose, to make thee a minister and a witness….To open their eyes, and to turn them from darkness to light, and

from the power of Satan unto God, that they may receive forgiveness of sins, and inheritance among them which are sanctified by faith.

He points out that referring to "the sanctified" as a past act already accomplished lends support to the fact that sanctification is an instantaneous experience, with a "before" and an "after."

Please notice that every time any of the apostles speak of people being sanctified, it is never by growth, but always by the power of God, and the act is always charged to the Father, the blood of the Son, or to the Spirit, and never to growth, death, the grave, or to resurrection.

Chapter Six
Humanity vs Carnality

Normal human nature is not sinful.   *That is, being a finite being endowed with choice is not sinful. Both the angels and Adam and Eve were such before falling into sin.*

No one goes very far in his Christian life until he finds that he has something in his nature that is not in accord with his desire to live for God and to keep His holy commandments.   *He shows different understandings of sanctification.*

(1) The Catholic Church teaches that this nature remains in us after conversion and that we cannot get rid of it here, but that after death the soul goes to purgatory and there it is refined and purified and made ready for heaven.

(2) (A) great many people of different Christian denominations...believe and teach that carnality is located in the physical or human body...(and therefore as) long as we live in the vessel of clay we will have to contend with carnality...(We) cannot be sanctified until we die.

(3) (A)nother group of fine people...teaches that carnality remains after the new birth and that we cannot get rid of it until death. They teach that we may be filled with the Holy

Ghost and have complete victory over the power of sin, or the old nature. They teach what is called the suppression of the evil nature.

(4) Next...I wish to mention the eradicationists, who are generally known as the "holiness people." They have always taught that (the) evil nature remains after conversion, but that it may be eradicated, or washed away, by the blood of Christ subsequent to the new birth.

Holiness people...do not use this term (i.e., *entire sanctification*) to mean full maturity, but they use it to mean full cleansing from sin and its pollution.

Holiness does not mean the absence of weakness, but it does mean the freedom from carnality and sin. Normal human nature is weak: it is not sinful. When it becomes sinful, it is then abnormal. Human beings in their normal state have appetites and inclinations which are wholly within the rights of every child of Adam. They are a part of us. Without them we would be abnormal. It is not a sin to have them, but it is a sin to use them illegally. God has taught in His Word how to use all of our human faculties to stay within the law. They are holy. To stop short of or go beyond the law is sin. To desire or to gratify our inclinations regardless of God's will or law is carnality.

Chapter Seven
Purity Vs. Maturity

Purity and maturity—these words are similar in sound, but they are very different in meaning. Purity may be found in the earliest moments after the soul finds pardon and peace with God through faith in His Son. Maturity is quite different, and is always obtained by growth, trial, and development over a period of time. The pure Christian may even be a weak Christian. It is not size or strength that is emphasized in sanctification, but only the absence of evil and the presence of elementary good. Purity is obtained as a crisis; maturity comes as a gradual process.

Growth is addition; purification is subtraction.

The perfection of holiness is entirely external. It means to bring every thought, word, and deed into complete accord with the spirit and principles of holiness within us. One cannot get purer than pure. There comes a time when our moral nature is made holy and the work is complete. However, there will always be room for improvement in our external lives...As we grow in grace and in knowledge, we are better able to bring our lives into a more beautiful conformity to the will of God.

Chapter Eight
Perfection: The Meaning of Perfection

The word "perfect" is used in the Scriptures with at least three different meanings.

First, there is the perfection of the moral or spiritual relationship with God or perfect love (Mt 5:48; 1 Jn 4:17f).

Second, there is the perfection of maturity, which means "come to age, or full grown": "We speak wisdom among them that are perfect" (1 Cor 2:6), and again, "Till we all come in the unity of the faith, and of the knowledge of the Son of God, unto a perfect man, unto the measure of the stature of the fullness of Christ" (Eph 4:13).

Third, there is a resurrection or eternal perfection. Thus Paul writes: "If by any means I might attain unto the resurrection of the dead. Not as though I had already attained, either were already perfect" Phil 3:11,12.

It is to be noted that Paul was pressing toward this resurrection perfection and said he was not perfect in that sense, (yet) he testified that he and others of these Philippian Christians were enjoying a perfection of some kind, for he said: "Let us therefore, as many as be perfect, be thus minded" (Phil 3:15). He was not perfect in the resurrection or eternal sense, but was perfect in his spiritual relation to God.

The third meaning of perfection: resurrection, or eternal perfection, is the eternal good of the Christian. The first meaning, or perfect love, is now the gracious privilege of the Christian in the experience of entire sanctification by faith in Christ. The second meaning, or maturity in grace, is the goal of progress for the Christian as he continues in the life of holiness.

Chapter Nine
Concluding Remarks

Why do not people get wholly sanctified when they are converted or born again? ....All the promises of God are on conditions...(T)here are certain conditions required of those who seek to get sanctified, (which) cannot be met until they are justified; therefore, sanctification invariably comes after justification. For example, to get sanctified wholly, it is required that one consecrate himself fully to the Lord; but a sinner cannot consecrate (himself) until he has repented of his sins.

He explains that when the word "sanctify" means "to separate," it refers to the believer's part, and that when the word means "to cleanse," it refers to God's activity of instantaneous sanctification

1. **THE BELIEVER'S PART**: "sanctify" equals "separate": Lev. 26:7, Ex. 28:41;29:43f; 30:28f; Num. 11:18; Jos. 3:5; Joel 1:14; Jn 17:17; Eph. 5:25,27; Heb. 9:13,14; 2 Tim. 2:21; Ex. 19:10; 2 Ch. 29:5, 15-19; Ac 15:8,9; Lev. 30:6.

2. **GOD'S PART**: "sanctify" equals "cleanse": 1 Th. 5:23; Heb. 2:11; 13:12; Jude 1; Rom. 15:16; 2 Th. 2:13; 1 Peter 1:2; 1 Th. 4:3; Heb. 10:9f; Ac 26:18; Heb 10:15. ❖

My Love Shall Steadfast Be

As long as sea tides flow,
   and birds fly to and fro,
As long as I shall know,
   I promise love to thee;
And when at break of dawn,
   the sun doth light its own,
My love shall steadfast be---
   to thee.

As long as suns do rise
   and set in golden skies,
As long as I realize,
   I promise love to thee;
Till seasons change no more,
   and life has closed the door,
My love shall steadfast be---
   to thee.

Though all the ivy fall
   from off the garden wall,
And will not grow at all,
   I promise love to thee;
Though stars refuse to shine,
   you shall be always mine:
My love shall steadfast be---
   to thee.

Written in the 1960s, to and for my wife, Virginia.

MEEKNESS [1]

To begin, I would like to say two things about "the fruit of the Spirit" in general. First, the term "Fruit of the Spirit" refers to that work which God through the Spirit is working *in* us to make us like Jesus---to conform us to the image of His Son (Rom 8:29). As Pentecostals we get excited about what God does *through* us---what Scripture calls the "gifts," healings, miracles, prophesies, etc. God does want to work *through* us, but he also wants to work *in* us, a process Paul describes in these words, "And we all, with unveiled face, beholding the glory of the Lord, are being changed into His likeness from one degree of glory to another" (2 Cor 3:18). The Spirit of the Living God is in process of transforming us into the likeness of Jesus Christ, our Lord, as we behold His beauty and glory.

A second general observation is this: The word "fruit" is in the singular, not the plural. There is an organic unity to the fruit of the Spirit and to Christian character. Therefore, we cannot pick and choose what we want, such as love, joy and peace, and bypass patience, meekness and temperance. As the prism breaks the shaft of light into a rainbow of colors, so Scripture reveals the beautiful components of the fruit of the Spirit. The same Spirit who produces peace also produces patience as we allow Him to work in us.

---

[1] This was one of nine presentations on the "Fruit of the Spirit," based on Gal 5:22f, given in a meeting of the Board of Church Ministries. The participants were: Carl H. Richardson (Love); W. A. Davis (Joy), Jim O. McClain, Sr. (Peace), Horace S. Ward (Long-Suffering), Lewis J. Willis (Kindness-Gentleness), O. W. Polen (Goodness), Raymond E. Crowley (Faith), James M. Beaty (Meekness) and W. J. (Bill) Brown (Temperance)

The quality of meekness, as described by the adjective 'meek,' is predicated of our Lord, both in his own words "Take my yoke upon you, and learn from me; for I am gentle (meek) and lowly in heart" (Mt 11:28), and in the words of the prophet, "Behold your king is coming to you humble (meek) and mounted on an ass (Mt 21:5; Zech 9:9). Also meekness is enjoined on us as His disciples (Mt 5:3; Eph 4:2, etc.).

What is meekness? In popular thinking, it often suggests "weakness". In fact Friedrich Nietzsche (1844-1900) called it "slave morality' and said that the Hebrew-Christian morality was perverted at this point. He advocated a morality of power; "might makes right."[2]

But meekness is not rooted in weakness and inability to help oneself, for Christ is meek. It is rooted in creatureliness and in Christ it refers to that humbling of Himself---that divine self-giving which we call the Incarnation, the laying aside of pre-rogative and submission of self unto death. Psalm 8 epitomizes the theology of man, the creature, in a prayer of adoration to the Creator, who is Lord of all. It speaks of the insignificance of man, "What is man that you are mindful of him?" But it also speaks of the significance of man, "Yet you have made him little less than the angels and crowned him with glory and honor...(and) made him to have dominion over the works of your hand."

Meekness has to do with a person's recognition of creatureliness and more specifically, of the limitations of that creatureliness. It is a by-product of faith, wrought by the Spirit, and is one aspect of one's self-image vis-à-vis God and others. As Vine says, "It is that temper of spirit in which we accept (God's) dealing with us as good, and therefore without disput-

---

[2] See Walter Kaufman, "Friedricih Nietzche" in the *Encyclopedia Americana* (Danbury, CO: Grolier, 2000), p. 327f, as well as similar articles in other encyclopedias.

ing or resisting."[3]   And it is negatively, he continues, "the opposite to self-assertiveness and self-interest; it is equanimity of spirit that is neither elated nor cast down, simply because it is not occupied with self at all."

We can characterize meekness by paraphrasing Paul, "Meekness is not thinking of oneself more highly than one ought to think, but thinking with sober judgment, according to the measure of faith which God has assigned to each one" (Rom 12:3).   Meekness, then, is faith maintaining the proper tension between one's insignificance and one's significance, so that one falls neither into an inferiority complex nor into a superiority complex.

In applying meekness to us, we should remember that God, through his Word, calls us to live our life and fulfill our ministry "with lowliness and meekness, with patience, forbearing one another in love, eager to maintain the unity of the Sprit in the bond of peace" (Eph 4:2f).

---

[3] W. E. Vine, *A Comprehensive Dictionary of Original Greek Words with their precise meanings for English readers* (Old Tappan, NJ: Fleming H. Revell, 1966), Vol. III, p. 55.

෨ ✝ ෬

Killed in Action

So simple--yet so stern---
So plain---but all too true--
Words of strict formality
Untouched by human emotions;
Yet behind them are tender feelings,
Pain, and anguish
Not conveyed by words.

"Killed in action" --Can it be?
Wake or sleep I? Dream or live?
Horrible reality that moves my being
To depths not felt before.
I would forget and dream,
But reality is too persistent.

---

෨ ✝ ෬

"Killed in Action" was written in 1944, after hearing the news
that a classmate had been killed. This was World War II; I was
nineteen, in my second year at college, studying for the ministry. The news of classmates dying added a depth of determina-
tion and consecration to the call of God to the ministry. This
poem appeared in *America Sings,* the first *Annual Anthology of
College Poetry*, published by the National Poetry Association,
Los Angeles, California, in 1944. It was also published in *The
Torchlight*, (Vol. II No. 5, p. 11, January, 1945) the school paper of Atlantic Christian College (now Barton College) in Wil-
son, NC.

THEOLOGY AND ETHICS
The Church of God Practical Commitments
The Other Half of Theology [1]

The topic which we have chosen for our first annual Theological Institute is: Theology and Ethics: the Church of God Practical Commitments. At the very beginning we thought it would be appropriate to give an overview of the structure and format of the conference and what is projected as its purpose and what we hope to achieve.

But first of all it will be helpful to define, or attempt to define, or at least call attention to, the principal words involved in the title which we have chosen for this conference. I would remind us that the process of defining draws on two sources: (1) etymology, which has to do with origin and original meaning and (2) usage, which has to do with the present value of the currency. Etymology and original meaning give the initial impetus and thrust to a word; its actual meaning at any later time depends on what it is used to mean in that particular context. Thus usage predominates over etymology

I. Theology

Let us, then, look at the first word in our conference title, viz., "theology." It is composed from two Greek words θεός (theáhs) and λόγος (láh-gahs), meaning respectively "God" and "word." The two words are used together in Scripture as "the word of God;" but they are not joined together as one word in the New Testament. Such is found in first century Greek; *theologos* is used both in pagan religion and by Philo of Alexan-

---

[1] This was given at the Church of God Theological Seminary.

dria (a Jew) to mean "the person who speaks for God."[2] In the early church John the Revelator was called "John the theologos" or "John the theologian," because he had been the instrument for the communication of the Word of God. From the point of view of etymology we could define theology as "what the word of God says" about some specific theme.

Now let us look at present-day usage for a definition of theology. We could say that theology (1) embodies the corporate vision of the church or a segment of the church (2) as to the truth and inter-relationship of the different aspects of the historic Christian faith. There is a strong current of overly exaggerated individualism in Western culture, and this influences theology and the doing of theology in the West. We speak of the theology of Luther, the theology of Calvin, and the theology of Wesley, but the value of any of these is augmented to the extent that the writer is able to capture the vision of the universal church and to articulate the historic Christian faith, while it is diminished to the extent that the writer explicates a privatized vision and either deletes or distorts the historic Christian faith.

Karl Barth defined dogmatics (or theology) as follows:

> Dogmatics is the science in which the Church, according to the present state of its knowledge, expounds the content of its message, critically, that is, measuring it by means of the Sacred Scriptures and being guided by its Confessional Writings.[3]

A word would be in order about how theology or the historic faith is distorted, in other words, how theology becomes heresy. Heresy is never of "whole cloth" or one-hundred percent false. Heresy generally arises from some "value" which a convert brings over into Christianity from a previous culture, relig-

---

[2] See Bauer-Arndt-Gringrich (BAG), *A Greek-English Lexicon of the New Testament* (Chicago: University of Chicago Press, 1960, p.356.

[3] Karl Barth, *Bosquejo de Dogmática* (Outline of Dogmatics), tr. by M. Gutierrez-Marin (Buenos Aires: La Aurora, 1954}, p. 15. The above passage was translated by the writer.

ion or philosophy. It may, in one sense, be a minor "error," but it can become pivotal and give a slant to the entire theological understanding of that person. Thus it was with the first heresy of the Church, that of the Judaizers. Having lived all their lives in Judaism, having been circumcised before faith and having observed the Law of Moses both before and after faith, they insisted that converts from among the Gentiles be circumcised and keep the Law.

Thus it was inevitable that distortions should occur when the Christian faith was introduced into the pagan world with its varied philosophical values. If one really believes that the material universe is evil, it is next to impossible to believe in the incarnation of the Word; and even though strong emphasis is placed on the divinity of Christ, what one ends up with is a "phantom" Christ who seems to be human but is not.

We would do well, however, to remember that Scripture distinguishes between heresy and damnable heresy, both in our relationship to so-called heretics and in our own understanding of the Christian faith in the light of the fact that we ourselves are not omniscient and many of us may, in fact, be in some measure of error in the way we understand some aspect of theology.

Thus we can say that theology encompasses the whole area of God's revelation in His Word and that it embodies a corporate or shared vision of the whole church or some part thereof. It is not a privatized vision, although at certain points in the history of the church, God has used individual messengers to call His people back to Himself and back to the truth.

II. Ethics

Now let us look at ethics. Ethics as a field of intellectual inquiry has been, and is, pursued either as a field of philosophy

or as a field of theology; and these have been known, respectively, as philosophical ethics and theological ethics. The word
ethics, itself, comes from the Greek word ἔθος (éh-thos),
meaning (1) habit, usage and (2) custom, law.[4] In usage ethics
has had to do, in both ancient and modern times, with the matter of right and wrong or good and evil and with moral duty
and obligation.

Ancient Greek philosophy, which was named the "love of
wisdom," proposed to investigate and organize all that can be
known about reality. In general, this was without reference to
a god or gods. The fields covered were many, metaphysics,
epistemology, logic, aesthetics, ethics, etc. Epistemology dealt
with "the nature and grounds of knowledge."[5] Logic dealt with
"the normative, formal principles of reasoning" or "the canons
and criteria of validity of inference and demonstration."[6] Aesthetics dealt with "the nature of the beautiful and with judg-
ments about the beautiful."[7] Metaphysics was so named first
by Aristotle in a treatise named "Metaphysika", that is, "after
or beyond" the physical. Metaphysics dealt with ontology (the
nature of being) and cosmology (the nature of the universe as
an orderly system). As we have already seen, ethics dealt with
the nature of right and wrong, or moral obligation, and was in
each system of philosophy correlated to its metaphysics or
view of ultimate reality. In other words there were two interre-
lated questions with which philosophy grappled, viz., (1) What
is the nature of ultimate reality? (metaphysics) and (2) In the
light of this ultimate reality, how should a person live? (ethics).

Take Epicurianism for an example: Epicurus, the founder,
adopted the metaphysics of Democritus, viz., that matter is
eternal and in perpetual motion; that motion and chance explain how things came to be as they are. The ethic which ra-

[4] BAG, p. 217.
[5] *Webster's Seventh New Collegiate Dictionary* (Springfield: G. & C. Merriam, 1967), p. 280.
[6] *Ibid.*, p. 497
[7] *Ibid.*, p. 15.

tionally follows is this: since there is no reality beyond the physical, that is, there is no god, no after-life, no accountability in the beyond, pleasure is the guide for all action in this world. If it feels good, do it. However, the philosophy did remind its adherents that there may be a "hang-over" or a "morning-after" and that this should be taken into account.

From this we see that in philosophy, ethics relates to the metaphysical presuppositions of the overall system or, stated in other words, that the basic presuppositions laid down about ultimate reality have logical and necessary consequences for the practical actions of those who adopt such a system.

Now for a look at theological ethics: there is, first of all, a major similarity and a major dissimilarity between philosophical ethics and theological ethics. The similarity is that in both there is, of necessity, a strong, logical connection between ethics and the fundamental presuppositions held about ultimate reality. The dissimilarity, however, is this: whereas in philosophy, an autonomous, abstract principle is adopted and applied to a concrete situation to give an ethical answer; in theology, not only is the understanding of the nature of ultimate reality obtained from the Word of the Living God, but so also is the understanding of moral duty. Thus it is a matter of obedience to God, through the commandment, and not just the application of a moral principle. "Love thy neighbor as thyself" is an imperative which requires obedience, and the obedience is to Him who gave the command. In any given instance when we are faced with the neighbor, we may ask, "How am I to love my neighbor?" At that point, due to the temptation of self, or as the New Testament calls it, the "flesh," we generally have a tendency to treat the commandment as a principle; that is, we are tempted to depersonalize it and to switch from an I-Thou encounter with the Giver of the commandment to an I-It relationship with the commandment. In this case, the "I" seeks to take command, to apply the commandment and to become "lord" over "it" (now seen as a principle), instead of remaining subject under the "Thou" and His commandment.

James Muilenberg, a Jewish scholar, speaking about the difference between ethics in Greek philosophy and duty as understood in Judaism, said that if we mean by ethics what the Greeks meant by ethics, viz., a rational, autonomous principle of action, then Judaism knows nothing of ethics. But if we mean, Does the Jew know what he is supposed to do? The answer is "Yes"; and he knows when and where he was told what to do it and who told him. This brings into sharp contrast the dissimilarity between philosophical and theological ethics.

III. Church of God Practical Commitments

Now let us give our attention to the phrase: Church of God Practical Commitments. Briefly, the history out of which these came is this: Elder Richard Spurling, at the strong urging of his son, Richard Green Spurling, organized, on August 19, 1886, a small congregation on Barney Creek (Monroe County, Tennessee), which took the name of Christian Union. Two weeks later the son was ordained and installed as the pastor of the small congregation.[8]

Over the next ten years Spurling continued to pastor the small congregation, and organized two or three other small groups and served as their pastor. During that time Sputling relocated twice and continued faithful in face of much opposition. By 1896 Spurling was living in Turtletown, Tennessee, close to the North Carolina border. That summer a very successful holiness meeting was held at the Shearer Schoolhouse, just across the line in North Carolina. Spurling and some of his congregation probably attended..

---

[8] The father, who was seventy-six in 1886, died in 1892. The son had needed the father, who was an ordained Baptist minister, to organize the little group, because he, the son, at the time had no credentials. He had been a licensed Baptist minister, but had given up hiss credentials two years previously and had worked with the Methodists.

On May 15, 1902 Spurling, in order to salvage some of the results of the revival of 1886, organized a congregation in the home of W. F. Bryant in Camp Creek, Cherokee County, North Carolina, and it was called the Holiness Church. A year later, on June 13, 1903, Ambrose Jessup Tomlinson joined the Holiness Church in Camp Creek and became the pastor and an active colleague of Richard G. Spurling and W. F. Bryant. At that time he was a home missionary from Indiana, living in Culberson, North Carolina, running a school for children in his home and doing colportage work in the mountains of Appalachia.

In December of the following year (1904) Tomlinson moved to Cleveland, Tennessee, in order to have access to better transportation and a larger outreach for ministry. On January 26 and 27, 1906, an Assembly was held in the home of J. C. and Malissa Murphy in Camp Creek. Since A. J. Tomlinson was the best prepared minister in the group and titular-pastor of the Camp Creek Church, he was asked to moderate. The next year (1907 at Union Grove outside Cleveland) the name of the church was changed to "Church of God." In March of 1910 the church began to publish a bi-weekly paper entitled *The Evening Light and Church of God Evangel*. The issue of August 15, 1910 was dedicated to the teachings of the Church and contained a list of twenty-five "Church of God Teachings." This was composed by a committee, consisting of A. J. Tomlinson, M. S. Lemmons, R. G. Spurling and T. L. McLain, as a guide for examining persons for the ministry.

The last two in this list of Teachings were apparently statements against Adventist doctrine. These were listed simply as:

24. Meats and drinks:
     Rom. 14:2-17; 1 Cor. 8:8; 1 Tim. 4:1-5.
25. The Sabbath:
     Hosea 2:11; Rom. 14:5f; Col. 2:16f; Rom. 13:1f.

The two teachings before these were the core and the beginning of our list of practical teachings. They were:

22. Total abstinence from all liquor or strong drinks:
    Prov. 20:1; 23:29-32; Isa. 28:7; 1 Cor. 6:10; Gal. 5:21.
23. Against the use of tobacco in any form, opium, morphine, etc.:
    Isa. 55:2; 1 Cor. 10:31f; 2 Cor. 7:1; Eph. 5:3-8; Jas. 1:21.

The stated purpose of the list was to assist candidates for ordination. The list was presented to the next General Assembly, and with a very minor change, it was adopted.

Over the years the list grew; some items were added and stayed, and some were added and later deleted. After a suggestion from the missionary leaders of South America in 1966, the Teachings were divided into (1) Doctrinal Commitments and (2) Practical Commitments by action of the General Assembly, in 1974.[9] In this form our Doctrinal Commitments very nearly parallel our Declaration of Faith.

In the Church of God, we are now[10] engaged in the study of our practical commitments. There is a widely felt need for improvement. Many items in the list need to be restated; there may be a consensus to leave some items out; and for sure there is a need to make the statement more comprehensive. And let us tell it like it is, some people would like to see the whole list eliminated.

At this point we could, and probably should, ask ourselves, "Why not?" The answer, which is to be found in Scripture, is that a holy and moral God requires a holy and moral life from His people. More specifically, the covenant creates obligations.

In preparation for this conference, the Lord gave me some new light on the Great Commission as it is found in Matthew 28:18-20, where it consists of five lines:

> All power (authority) is given unto me
>   in heaven and in earth.

---

[9] 55th General Assembly Minutes, p. 51.
[10] That is, at the time this lecture as written and delivered.

Go ye therefore, and teach (disciple) all
   nations,
baptizing them in the name of the Father,
   and of the Son, and of the Holy Ghost:
teaching them to observe all things
   whatsoever I have commanded you:
and lo, I am with you always,
   even unto the end of the world. Amen.

Over the years I had become aware that the baptismal for-mula, which also served as a confessional formula for the can-didate who was to be baptized, did, in the process of time, de-velop into the Apostles' Creed. "Thou are the Christ, the Son of the living God" may have been an adequate confession of faith within Judaism, but once evangelization began among the Greeks, attention had to be given also to God the Father and God the Holy Spirit. Little by little the baptismal formula of Matthew, which is repeated in the *Didache*, was expanded into the Creed. It was called a creed because, in Latin, it began, *Credo* (I believe).

The late Jewish scholar Martin Buber made a distinction be-tween "believe in," which, he said, characterizes the Jewish faith, and "believe that," which, he said, characterizes the Christian faith.[11] The truth is that Biblical faith in both testa-ments contains both of these aspects of faith. The faith that Jahweh is the true and living God and that He brought Israel out of bondage and that He made them His people in a special covenant-making event at Sinai is just as germane and crucial to Judaism as the faith that God sent His Son, Jesus Christ, who died and rose again is for the Christian faith. And both covenants require that God's people trust in him. Faith in Yahweh and faith in the Lord Jesus Christ is, in the respective covenants, the living link between God and His people who are in covenant with Him.

---

[11] Martin Buber, *Two Types of Faith* (NY: Harper and Row, 1961).

Moreover, it is the "faith that" in Scripture which makes a creed possible, and, we might say, even necessary. Out of the baptismal, confessional creed, theology, as we generally think of it, developed. Three factors aided this process: (1) the periodic rise of heresies and the felt need of the church to answer these; (2) the questions and accusations from the outside culture, especially those from philosophy; and (3) the organizing mind of church leaders under the influence of Greco-Roman culture.

The theology which developed in this way became very intellectual and abstract, especially after it became heavily influenced by philosophy. Those who produced it assuredly supposed that they were basing their theology on the Word of God, and in one sense they were--but only on one aspect of it: that which reveals the truth about the different "heads" or topics of theology, whatever these may turn out to be in one's system, such as God, man, sin, redemption, Christ, Holy Spirit and things to come. In other words theology turned out to be mainly about the indicative and not about the imperative.

Parallel to this, and almost lost to the eyes of the modern church, was the development which resulted from the fourth line of the Great Commission, viz., "teaching them to observe all things whatsoever I have commanded you." This speaks of three things: (1) there are things which have been commanded by the Lord; (2) these things must be observed by the baptized; and (3) these things should be taught to new converts, for the most part, before water baptism. To be honest, my attention had never before focused beyond the first two words of this line, viz., "teaching them..." I had supplied, from my own imagination, something like "correct doctrine" in order to complete the idea. But the teaching mandated here is different from the teaching of the credo, which could perhaps be called a theology of the truth. This is a theology of life, that is, what the Word of God says about how to live the Christian life.[12]

The Word says a lot more about this than most of us, as yet, have seen. Much of the teaching of Jesus falls into this category. The so-called paraenetic passages of the epistles contain this teaching.[13] In fact, the treatises of James, I Peter and I John are practically all paraenesis. ❖

The following was also a part of the original paper.

The purpose of this First Annual Theological Institute is to look at, and to examine in depth, this other side of theology. We decided to open the Institute tonight with a celebration of our unity around the Lord's Table and in the washing of the saints' feet. Tomorrow we have scheduled three workshops to look at three important areas: the Biblical area, the historical area and the theological area. Following these there will be a case study in which we will have the opportunity to grapple with the specifics of a concrete case. Tomorrow night there will be a Panel Discussion by some of the members and consultants of the committee who drew up the new proposed statement on Practical Commitments, and our General Overseer will give us a report on the studies which are now under way on the Practical Commitments.

On Tuesday morning from 8:00 to 9:15 there will be two simultaneous workshops, and from 9:30 to 10:45 there will be two more simultaneous workshops. The four workshops will incorporate all of the regular classes scheduled before Chapel on Tuesday. We will close the conference with a special Chapel service from 11:00 to noon, in which there will be an attempt to sum up and focus what we have accomplished.

---

[12] The rabbis by this time had also developed two "branches" of study: Haggadah (inspirational/motivational) and Hallakah (how to walk, i.e., how to live as a Jew).

[13] The paraenetic passages teach us how to live, as Christians, and exhort or encourage us to put those things into practice.

I have great hopes and expectations for this conference and pray that God will use it to bless His people. ✤

꽃

THE BIBLICAL VIEW OF SEX [1]

Have you not read:
He who made them from the beginning
made them male and female?...
Therefore, what God has joined together,
let no one put asunder.
Jesus (Mt 19:4,6)

In our day when sex is perverted, abused, and misused in every way conceivable, it behooves us as Christians to search the Scriptures in order to know where we are called to stand if we are to discern and understand properly the true nature of our own sexuality.

When Jesus was questioned about the possibility of a man divorcing his wife for any reason whatsoever, he explained that Moses had permitted certain things to the children of Israel because of the hardness of their hearts; but he also pointed his disciple back to the purposes of God as manifested in the creation "at the beginning." This gives us warrant to try to discover in creation those purposes, structures, and orders that God established for the human race, prior to the entrance of sin and rebellion against the Creator. There are at least three of these that concern human sexuality.

---

[1] *Church of God Evangel*, (Vol. 59, No. 31) October 13, 1969, pp. 5,6,7,20; revised.

THE ORDER OF CREATION

The Body: The Wholeness of the Human Being

A human being, although more than just a physical being in a physical universe, still had a physical, concrete and material linkage to the space-time continuum which we call creation. "The Lord God formed man of the dust of the ground, and breathed into his nostrils the breath of life; and man became a living soul" (Gen 2:7).

This means two things: (1) In the **first place** it means that God gave us, by means of our very constitution, a parable of our dependence on Him. The body must be nourished and re-plenished from the physical universe. We do not live in, of and out of ourselves; our life is received and must be renewed and maintained. We are dependent on our "daily bread" and the air that we breathe. And yet the mystery of the maintenance of life is not to be explained only by this physical dependence on the material universe: "Man shall not live by bread alone, but by every word that proceeds from the mouth of God."[2] God is our true source of life; when we are cut off from that source, death begins. (2) In the **second place** it means that we are con-stituted, as God tells us in His Word and shows us in death, of both the physical and the nonphysical, of the visible and the invisible, or as Paul says, referring to these two dimensions, the outer being and the inner being.

The body is the outer being (person) and serves as the instru-ment of the inner being (person), both for the service of God to our fellow human beings and for the dominion of creation. In Scripture the body is not evil, as in Greek thought. On the con-trary, the source of corruption is the heart, the rebellious will-- the inner person. The body is good. However, in general, Scripture is concerned with the totality of the human being.

---

[2] Jesus in Mt 4:4, citing Dt 8:3.

The Duality of the Sexes: Male and Female

He who made them at the beginning made them male and female" (Mt 19:4). After the Lord had made the man, He said, "It is not good that the man should be alone; I will make him an help meet for him" (Gen 2:18). Woman was created as a helper, a partner, a fellow worker to stand over against man in an I-thou relationship "fit for him" as a "mirror of himself in which he recognizes himself."[3] Male and female stand over against each other in a way that is mutually dependent and complementary, "a polarity which is constitutive of man as such. Therefore man and woman do not find each other, as it were, subsequently; they rather come to each other from each other."[4] Sexuality then is a gift of the Creator, whether life is lived out in the celibate state or in the married state (1 Cor 7:7).

Through the sex act the male and the female come to "know" each other, and thereby to know something of the secret of their own existence. The use of the term "know" as a synonym for sexual intercourse is not a matter of delicacy. Through sex one discovers something that one had not, from the inside, "known" before---something about another human being, and thus also something about him or herself,. The riddle of one's existence does not lie in the stars. Through one's physical existence the human being has received a gift that transcends the physical existence which is shared with animals. How this happens is a mystery. Sex is in some basic sense sacramental, in that a spiritual gift has emerged through a physical act. Sex is not apart from God. It is a part of God's creation.[5]

---

[3] F. Delitzsch, quoted by Helmut Thielicke, *The Ethics of Sex* (New York: Harper and Row, 1964), p. 4.

[4] Thielicke, *Ethics,* p 5.

[5] See Seward Hiltner, *Sex and the Christian Life* (New York: Association Press, 1957), pp. 35, 36.

One Flesh: Marriage

Therefore shall a man leave his father and his mother, and
shall cleave unto his wife: and they shall be one flesh" (Gen
2:24). "What, therefore, God has joined together, let no one
put asunder" (Mt 19:16). Marriage is grounded in the duality
of the sexes, which, itself, is a constituent part of the things
that were created and is therefore part of the order of creation.
This means that the status of marriage "in its original intention...was to be that of a partnership between man and woman
(Gen 2:18), a state of being created for each other (2:21f), and
of recognizing themselves in each other" (2:23).[6]

From the second chapter of Genesis through the remainder of
the Bible, there is reference to 'one-flesh' union. The two shall
become one flesh. The essential meaning of this, rightly noted
by the Anglican author D. S. Bailey, is that it has a radical
character, whether one is aware of this or not.

> What takes place is an organic rather than an arithmetical
> kind of union. It is a serious matter, for good or ill...in every
> case the character of the union will be determined by the
> character of its constitutive act!...Authentic union in 'one
> flesh' occurs, (Bailey says)...through 'intercourse following
> consent between a man and a woman who love one another
> and who act freely, deliberately, responsibly and with the
> knowledge and approval of the community, and in so doing
> (whether they know it or not) conform to the divine law.'[7]

One of the purposes of marriage is the bearing and rearing of
children. And procreation is accomplished, of course, through
the sex act or becoming "one flesh." But this is not the same
as saying, as some do, that the only purpose of sex is reproduc-
tion. Paul speaks of the conjugal rights of both husband and
wife and the fact that one does not rule over one's own body
but that one's spouse does. He goes on the say:

---

[6] Thielicke, p 105.
[7] Cited by Hiltner, pp. 47,48.

Do not refuse one another except perhaps by agreement for a season that you may devote yourselves to prayer and that you may 'then come together again,' lest Satan tempt you through lack of self-control (I Cor 7:3-5).

THE ORDER OF REDEMPTION

How One Sees Him or Herself

In the Christian faith, the body is not only the work of the Creator, but it is also redeemed, i.e., it is bought with a price. And when redeemed, it is the temple of the Holy Spirit and awaits resurrection, to be changed into the likeness of His glorious body for eternal service to our Lord and God. It makes a lot of difference what a Christian does with the body since it is not one's own in an absolute sense. It is this body that has received the gift of sexuality. In the body the differentiation of the duality of the sexes is manifested, and through the body and the possibility of "becoming one flesh," both the one and the other find fulfillment.

In Paul's First Letter to the Corinthians he discusses how we should look upon ourselves, including our bodies and our sexuality.

Now the body is not for immoral, sexual relations,
but for the Lord, and the Lord for the body.
And God, who raised the Lord,
will also raise us up by his power.
Do you not know:
Your bodies are members [organic parts] of Christ?
Shall I then take the members of Christ
and make them members of a prostitute? Never!
Do you not know:
When one joins himself to a prostitute
he becomes one body with her?
For it say, *The two shall become one flesh.*
But whoever is joined to the Lord
is one Spirit with him.

Flee from immoral sexual relations.
Every sinful deed that one may commit is outside the body;
but whoever commits immoral, sexual acts
sins against one's own body.
Do you not know...?
Your body is the temple of the Holy Spirit who is in you,
whom you have from God and you are not your own.
Because you were bought with a price.
So glorify God in your body.
  (I Cor 6:13-20, tr of author).

As believers we belong to the Lord. This is true in a threefold
way: we are His by creation; we are His by redemption, and we
are His by consecration (Rom 12:1). The body, as the physical
instrument of the self, is also His. It is His instrument (the or-
gans of His body since we are united to Him) and His dwelling
place by the Spirit. Therefore, God will destroy him who de-
stroys God's temple (See I Cor 3:17).

How One Sees His or Her Spouse

We should never use other persons as a 'means' to accomplish our own purposes. We should always consider and treat
them as 'ends' in themselves. Therefore persons should be re-
garded in relation to their 'being,' rather than in relation to
their 'function.' This is especially important in the marriage
relationship. The other person should always be seen as a gift
from God, a human being who is the object of God's love, both
through creation, as made in the image of God, and through
redemption, as one for whom Christ died.

  The desired body belongs to the 'being' of a human being who himself belongs to another; a human being, that
  is, who has been bought with a price (I Cor 6:20; 7:23)
  and has a temporal and eternal destiny, a destiny in
  which one who claims this other person in his totality re-
  sponsibly participates. Only through this meditation do
  we come to see that whole human being, who alone is

capable of disclosing the full richness of sexuality. For among the conclusions of our study will be the realization that focusing one's intention upon the whole man, upon his indivisible unity, does not merely curb sex, but rather liberates it and brings it to its fullness. He who sees only the partial--only the body, only the function, and again possibly only a part of this--remains unfulfilled even on the level of eros, because, having lost the wholeness of the other person, he also loses the other person's uniqueness.[8]

Because the marriage partner is such a person with an eternal destiny, toward whose eternal fulfillment we may be either a help or a hindrance, we must respect the dignity and mystery of his or her being and never use our spouse as a mere means to an end for oneself. Thus in the bonds of marriage my spouse becomes for me my "neighbor" (Near-One) under the sign of agape (love).

But just any 'near-one' will not do as a sexual partner in the institution of marriage. It must be one of the opposite sex, of appropriate age, type, and character, etc., who could stand in a complementary relationship to 'me'. It is in this relationship that *eros* (erotic love) comes into play, but where one is also obligated to manifest *agape*. "The person to whom I relate myself erotically must be my 'neighbor' and hence the object of my *agape*. Otherwise, I dehumanize him"[9].

Luther once defined the love of God as contrasted with human *eros* in this way: 'The love of God does not find that which is worthy of his love, but rather creates it for himself; but the love of man comes into being through the lovableness which it finds.'[10]

---

[8] Thielicke, pp. 24,25.
[9] Thielicke, p 34. *Eros* is never used in the New Testament, not even for even for love within marriage.
[10] Thielicke, p 97.

As C. S. Lewis put it, *eros* is need-love and *agape* is gift-love. *Eros* sees the companion as of value "for me" and *agape* sees him or her as of value "for God." *Eros* desires the other person. The lover is fascinated by the beloved, and it is not all chemistry. *Agape* wills the best for the beloved, the most complete fulfillment of his or her highest potential, the becoming of what he or she is called by God to become. Christian marriage needs both *eros* and *agape*.

POSTSCRIPT

The Demand of God in the Light of the Gift of Sexuality

In the light of the fact that God is the Creator and that He made us male and female, we should ask this question, "Is He concerned with how we use or express our sexuality?" Scripture makes it plain that God is concerned; and based on this fact, I have tried to explain some of the positive purposes of sex.

Does the Christian faith understand that God has set certain limits to the use and expression of sex? It does! As C. S. Lewis said, "The Christian rule is 'either marriage, with complete faithfulness to your partner or else total abstinence.'"[11] Both the married and the unmarried are called to Christian discipleship; the married are called to "fidelity within marriage"; and the unmarried are called to "continence outside of marriage." Or as Demant says, "Celibacy requires the suppression of all sexual experience and marriage the suppression of some."[12] The Apostle Paul wrote to the Church in Thessalonica,

> For this is the will of God, (even) your consecration [sanctification]: that you abstain from immorality; that each one of

[11] C. S. Lewis, *Mere Christianity* (London: Geoffrey Bles, 1953), Book III Christian Behaviour, Chapter 5. Sexual Morality, p 76.
[12] V. A. Demant, *Christian Sex Ethics* (New York: Harper and Row, 1963), p 35.

you know how to take a wife for himself in consecration [holiness] and honor, not in the passion of lust like (the) heathen who do not know God; that no man transgress and wrong his brother in this matter, because the Lord is an avenger in all these things as we solemnly forewarned you. For God has not called us for uncleanness, but in consecration [holiness] (I Th 4:3-7, RSV). ✠

References

V. A. Demant, *Christian Sex Ethics* (New York: Harper and Row, 1963).

Seward Hiltner, *Sex and the Christian Life* (New York: Association Press, 1957).

C. S. Lewis, *Mere Christianity* (London: Geoffrey Bles, 1953), Book III Christian Behaviour, Chapter 5. Sexual Morality

......*The Four Loves* (London: Collins, Fontana Books, 1963).

Helmut Thielicke, *The Ethics of Sex* (New York: Harper and Row, 1964).

ℰℜ
Born Babe of Bethelem

Born Babe of Bethelem, Born Emmanuel,
Word of God incarnate, come to earth to dwell,
Bearing truth and glory, God on earth to trod,
Come ye to Bethlehem, worship thy God!

Born Babe of Bethelem, Lamb of God was He,
Precious, sinless Son of God, come to die for thee,
Shepherds came to worship, saw what God had done;
Come ye to Bethlehem, worship the Son!

Born Babe of Bethlehem, King of Kings to be,
Humble birth of majesty, come to set men free,
Wise men came in splendor, gifts to Him did bring;
Come ye to Bethlehem, worship thy King!

Part Three

Christmas, Easter and Pentecost

THE MYSTERY OF THE INCARNATION [1]

And the Word was made flesh and dwelt among us...
full of grace and truth.
Jn 1:14

Christmas is a time when we remember and celebrate the fact that God loved the world and sent his only begotten Son to be our Savior. The only accounts that we have of this royal birth are found in the Gospel of Matthew, written from Joseph's point of view, and in the Gospel of Luke, written from Mary's point of view.

The mystery of the Incarnation rests in the person of Jesus Christ. Christ was God and man during the time of his life in the flesh. The word "mystery" in the Scriptures refers to that which a human being could never find out by one's own investigation, but something that God has revealed. Once it has been revealed, it is logical to people of faith, even though they do not understand it in its totality.

If God had not revealed it, the natural human being could never have perceived the fact that Jesus of Nazareth was both God and man. But now that it has been revealed, we see this truth and we understand it by faith, even though it is shocking to the mind of man.

Returning to the story of his birth, if this child is really both God and man, then his existence did not begin with his conception and birth; only his human dimension began there. He ex-

---

[1] Published in Spanish in *El Evangelio,* Vol. 28, No 12, December, 1973, pp 4-6. Translated by the author.

isted forever as the eternal Son of God. Thus the weak, sweet child Jesus is the mighty, eternal Son of God. At Christmas time we have the tendency to exaggerate the infantile aspect of Jesus, the child. But He whom we behold in the manger is the eternal Creator.

> *All things were made by Him, and without Him,*
> *nothing was made that was made.*   **Jn 1:3**
> *For in Him all things were created,*
> *whether in heaven or on earth,*
> *whether visible and invisible;*
> *whether thrones or dominions,*
> *or principalities or powers;*
> *all things were made by Him and for Him.*   **Col 1:16f**

Therefore his preexistence was and is a dimension of the incarnation that the natural mind could never have discovered. When he said, "Before Abraham was I am" (Jn 8:58), the unbelieving Jews said that he was a Samaritan and that he had a demon (Jn 8:48,52).

How could the preexistent Son of God come to be Mary's child? It was through what believers have come to call 'the virgin birth.' And this is part of the revelation also. This is so interwoven into the texture of both Matthew and Luke that no kind of textual criticism or reinterpretation can take it out. Honesty demands an admission that the virgin birth is the very essence of the only two inspired accounts that we have of his birth.

In the Gospel of Matthew, when Joseph discovered that Mary "was with child," he was troubled. But the Lord, in a vision and through his angel, said to him, "That which is conceived in her is of the Holy Spirit. And she shall bring forth a son, and you shall name him Jesus, because he will save his people from their sins" (Mt 1:18-21). The Holy Spirit inspired Matthew to write that this was the fulfillment of what had been spoken by the Lord through his prophet, saying, "Behold, a virgin shall conceive, and give birth to a son, and his name shall be called 'Emmanuel,' which in translation is 'God with us' ((Isa 7:14 & Mt 1:23).

In Luke's account, which clearly comes from Mary, the angel Gabriel made the announcement to Mary in these word,

Behold, you shall conceive in your womb, and bring forth a son, and you shall call his name 'Jesus'. He shall be great, and shall be called the Son of the Most High; and the Lord God shall give him the throne of his father David. And he shall reign over the house of Jacob for ever and his kingdom shall never end (1:31-33).

The first reaction of Mary was, "How can this be, since I do not know a man?" And the answer was, "The Holy Spirit shall come on you, and the power of the Most High shall over-shadow you; therefore, also that holy being, which shall be born, shall be called the Son of God." (Lk 1:35)

Today, because of pressure from so-called "scientific study," many people do not want to believe in the Virgin birth. But, after careful study of both Matthew and Luke, one ought, in all honesty, to admit that, no matter how we translate the word 'virgin,' the truth of the virgin birth is a part of both accounts. Personally, if I believed that Jesus was born in the normal way through intercourse of a man and a woman, I could not believe that he was, in any way, the preexistent Son of God.

We have already mentioned that the mystery of the incarnation is rooted in the person of Jesus Christ, i.e., in the fact that he was both God and man. One of the most important aspects of this mystery concerns the purpose of the incarnation. In other words, why is it that "God so loved the world that he gave his only begotten Son?" And the answer is, "that all who believe in him should not perish, but have everlasting life" (Jn 3:16); and "that the world might be saved through him" (Jn 3:17). In the prologue to his Gospel, John says,

And the Word was made flesh and dwelt among us...full of
grace and truth...(so that)..whoever received him--even
those who believe on his name--(might be given) the power[2]
to become the sons of God (Jn 1:14,12).

In other words the purpose of the incarnation is redemption.

The Apostle Paul states the purpose of the coming of Christ
beautifully in these words, "For you know the grace of our
Lord Jesus Christ, that, though he was rich, yet for your sakes
he became poor, that you through his poverty might be rich" (2
Cor 8:9). He was rich---from all eternity he shared the glory of
the Father---nevertheless he was born as a babe in Bethlehem
and laid in a manger, making himself poor by that very act.
But he drew near to us and finally gave his life so that we
might be raised up, made rich, i.e., be forgiven and receive everlasting life.

In another passage Paul describes "this mind" that was in
Christ Jesus, who, although he was "in the form of God," was
willing to lay aside his privileged position and to "take the
form of a servant, to be made in the likeness of man" and to
humble himself and to become "obedient unto death, even
death on a cross" (Phl 2:5-11). This is redemption; this is the
purpose of the incarnation.

The author of the Epistle to the Hebrews applies the words of
Psalm 8 to the Lord Jesus (ch. 2). The Psalmist, after viewing
the vastness of God's creation, especially the expanse of the
heavens, recognized, in contrast, the insignificance of mankind. But God also made the Psalmist to see the greatness of
man, which comes from the purpose of God for man (made
little lower than God[3], crowned with glory and honor, appointed by God to have dominion over the rest of creation).

---

[2] "Power" is the KJ translation. The word is ἐξουσία (*eks-ou-si-a*) and
means "authority" or "right."
[3] The Hebrew word here is *Elohim.* It is the generic term used to refer to
the Lord God and to the pagan gods. The Greek Septuagint translated it as
angels and this is followed in the King James.

The writer applied all of this to Christ, in these words, "But we see Jesus, who was made a little lower than the angels for the suffering of death, crowned with glory and honor, (so) that he, by the grace of God, should taste death for everyone" (2:9).

Then he goes on to say that Jesus did not come in the form of an angel, but took human form in order to die, and by his death, to liberate us from the slavery of death.

> Thus, since children share in flesh and blood, he himself also did the same, that through death he might destroy him who has the power of death, that is, the devil, and deliver all those who through fear of death were subject to lifelong bondage. For he, indeed, was not concerned to became an angel but to become a man, even one of the descendants of Abraham. Therefore he needed to be like his brothers in every respect, so that he might become a merciful and faithful high priest before God, to make expiation for the sins of the people. And since he himself has suffered and been tempted, he is able to help those who are tempted. (He 2:14-18)

Thus the Christ-child was born to die, not in the sense that all human beings are born to die (the inevitable), but he was born to die so that everyone else could live. Generally we do not associate his death with his birth---we reserve that for Holy Week. But the child of Bethlehem was born to be crucified, as the Lamb of God, offered from before the foundation of the world, to take away the sins of the world. Thus the joy of Christmas is a somber joy. Emmanuel has come, but he has come to die for us and our sins, so that we might live. The child is born! Hallelujah! But the path begun in the manger leads to the cross. His passion will be to do the will of his Father...to give his life as a ransom for all. "His hour," when it comes, will not only be the darkest hour, because he will be made sin and the Father will hide his face from him, but also, it will be the hour of his glorification, because he will fulfill that for which he came into the world.

The mystery of the incarnation looks back to the preexistence of the Son of God and the creation of all things, but also it looks ahead, to the cross and the work of redemption. "God was in Christ reconciling the world to himself" (2 Cor 5:18). "Thanks be to God for his unspeakable gift" (2 Cor 9:15)!

Great indeed is the mystery of godliness:
God was manifested in the flesh,
justified in the Spirit,
seen of angels,
preached to the nations,
believed on in the world,
received up into glory (1 Tm 3:16).

೫ ❀ ಜ
THE POWER OF HIS RESURRECTION [1]

If ye then be risen with Christ,
seek those things which are above.
Col 3:1
That I may know him,
and the power of his resurrection.
Phil 3:10.

How wonderful to serve the living Christ! He rose from the dead and lives for ever and ever. Only He could say, "I am he that liveth, and was dead; and, behold, I am alive for evermore. Amen" (Rev 1:18). The heart of the gospel is the crucifixion and resurrection of Jesus Christ. All that God has prepared for us is obtainable only through our identification with Christ in His crucifixion and resurrection.

Paul writes to the Colossians, "If ye then be risen with Christ, seek those things which are above ...set your affection on things above, not on things on the earth" (3:1). What are the "things above"--those things which we should seek and on which we should set our affections? We find at least a part of the answer in Paul's writings to the Philippians, "Yea ... I count all things but loss ...that I may know him, and the power of his resurrection" (3:8,10). This is what Paul's affection was set upon...Christ "and the power of his resurrection." Now what does the "power of his resurrection" mean? First, it refers to something that Paul could know; it also refers, quite evidently, to the power that was manifested at the resurrection of Christ. Let us look at these two things in chronological order.

---

[1] *Church of God Evangel* (Vol 47, No 4) March 26, 1956, pp. 5f.

Our day is a day that puts great importance on power and authority. Whether it is transportation, or communication, indus-
try or war, the demand is power and more power. At every
new demonstration of power, the world marvels. Yet it only
sees natural power and, many times, only the boisterous type of
that. One Sunday morning, nearly two thousand years ago,
there was a manifestation of spiritual power such as our old
world had never seen before. There was no deafening sound,
no binding light, no mushrooming cloud; but there was the
manifestation of "the exceeding greatness of his power..., the
working of his mighty power, which he wrought in Christ,
when he raised him from the dead" (Eph 1:19f). It was the
power of the Almighty God, breaking open the gates of hell
and death, tearing asunder the shackles of sin, and victoriously
bearing forth the keys of death and hell. It was the incarnate
Almighty coming forth from the regions of death, "because it
was not possible that he should be holden of it" (Ac 2:24). It
was He who was "declared to be the Son of God with power.
It was He who could say, "All power is given unto me in
heaven and in earth" (Mt 28:18).

The resurrection of Christ is different from other historical
events---the discovery of America, for example---in that it is
related to us, not only historically but also, as the basis for a
life-changing experience. Paul wrote to the Ephesians of his
>   making mention of you in my prayers;...That...God...may give
>   unto you the spirit of wisdom...The eyes of your understanding
>   being enlightened; that ye may know...what is the exceed-
>   ing greatness of his power to us-ward who believe, accord-
>   ing to the working of his mighty power, which he wrought
>   in Christ, when he raised him from the dead. (1:16-20)

So the power of His resurrection is great to work in those of us
who trust in him, both to will and to do. How then do we, or
can we, know the power of His resurrection?

We know the power of His resurrection initially in regeneration. The natural man is dead in sin. He is in the tomb of sin

and death. His only hope of resurrection is through the power of Christ's resurrection. Physical might, brilliant learning, scientific skill, and polished culture avail naught in imparting spiritual life to the natural man. But there is hope! "And you, being dead in your sins and the uncircumcision of your flesh, hath he quickened together with him, having forgiven you all trespasses" (Col 2:13). Yes, we were dead in sins, "But God, who is rich in mercy, for his great love wherewith he loved us, Even when we were dead in sins, hath quickened us together with Christ" (Eph 2:4f). Yes, the power that works in regeneration, bringing light and life and banishing darkness and death, is the power of His resurrection.

We shall know the power of His resurrection consummately in the day of the coming of our "Saviour, the Lord Jesus Christ: Who shall change our vile body, that it may be fashioned like unto his glorious body, according to the working whereby he is able even to subdue all things unto himself" (Phil 3:20f). For "if the Spirit of him that raised up Jesus from the dead dwells in you, he that raised up Christ from the dead shall also quicken your mortal bodies by his Spirit that dwelleth in you" (Rom 8:11). When? On that day for which all creation groaneth and for which "Even we ourselves groan within ourselves, waiting for the adoption, to wit, the redemption of our body" (Rom 8:23).

That day will be a day of power and glory! "For this corruptible must put on incorruption, and this mortal must put on immortality" (1 Cor 15:53). Then "we shall be like him; for we shall see him as he is" (1 Jn 3:2).

There is the story told of a missionary in the heart of Africa who was working at translating the Bible. He had an African Christian who spoke the language working with him. They came to the third chapter of 1 John.

Behold, what manner of love the Father hath bestowed upon us, that we should be called the sons of God: therefore the world knoweth us not, because it knew him not. Beloved,

now are we the sons of God, and it doth not yet appear what
we shall be: but we know that, when he shall appear, we
shall be like him; for we shall see him as he is. (3:1f)
At that point the assistant exclaimed, "But Pastor, this cannot
be right. It should say, 'When we see Him, we shall kiss His
feet.'" Then the missionary explained to him the bountifulness
and graciousness of the provision of our Lord and explained
that on that day of glory we shall really be like him. What a
blessed hope. "And every man that hath this hope in him puri-
fieth himself, even as he is pure" (1 Jn 3:1-3).

But having known the power of His resurrection in regeneration and hoping to know that power again in the resurrection of
the body, we have by no means exhausted the provisions of our
Heavenly Father.   Between these two events is the time in
which Paul desired "that I may know him and the power of his
resurrection." After regeneration, it is the power of His resurrection that is the secret of victorious living. It gives victory
over sin, the flesh and the world. It helps us overcome temptation and worry. That is the reason Paul could say, "I live, yet
not I, but Christ liveth in me" (Gal 3:20). When the risen
Christ dwells within, He makes available that resurrection
power. Our job is to avail ourselves of that power. How often
we wrestle and worry over the problems of life until we realize
that the living Son of God, the Master of every situation is
standing beside us and dwelling within us. If we would just
remember to seek Him first, how much less energy we would
expend fighting in our own strength and how much happier we
would be!

The power of His resurrection is also the secret of victorious
ministry. Paul, speaking of his ministry, wrote, "Whereunto I
also labor, striving according to his working, which worketh in
me mightily" (Col 1:29). May we all strive to be a channel of
power that He might work through us mightily! When Jesus
said, "All authority is given unto me in heaven and in earth.[2]

---

[2] The KJV has 'power'; the Greek reads 'authority' (ἐξουσία, ex-ou-SI-a).

Go ye therefore ..." (Mt 28:18f), it seems as though He was saying, and I think He was, "All authority is mine; I am making it available to you; go, and, as you go, use it to accomplish those things which I have sent you to do." A powerless ministry is an empty hull. Our prayer should be for a spiritual ministry of power.

At this and every Eastertide, let us think on and set our affections on "those things which are above;" and may it be our supreme desire that we may know "him in the power of his resurrection."

ഓ
Mary's Lullaby

O my child, sweet and mild, gift of the Father's love,
   How can it be that I hold you,
   When you hold all things in your hands!

Refrain:
Lullaby, sleep tonight; You are the glory of Israel;
Lullaby, sleep tonight, You are the light of the world.

O my child, sweet and mild, gift of the Father's love,
   How can it be that I feed you,
   When your are the source of all life!

O my child, sweet and mild, gift of the Father's love,
   How can it be that I clothe you,
   When you clothe the lilies so fair!

THE HOLY SPIRIT
His Presence and Power in the Church [1]

To a lot of people in our time, and even to many professed Christians, the Holy Spirit is of little significance. Along with picturing God in their minds as an old man with a beard, seated on a throne, and Jesus in terms of a man of some thirty-odd years, some people visualize the Holy Spirit as a fog or cloud, completely removed from our life and experience today.

Previous to the actual coming of the Holy Spirit on the Day of Pentecost, the disciples of Jesus seemed to be confused, as many people are today, about the Spirit and about what Jesus had said would happen at His coming. But in the light of what Jesus had taught them and of what they experienced that day, they began to understand things more clearly.

On the Day of Pentecost two things happened as a result of this inaugural coming of the Spirit. First, the Church as the body of Christ was constituted or formed, and secondly, each of those waiting for the promise was filled with, or baptized in, the Holy Spirit.

Extraordinary signs were manifested that day. There was a sound---it was like the rushing of a mighty wind (Ac 2:2); and there was a sight—it was like flames of fire, resting on each one of them (Ac 2:3). And after the infilling of the Spirit, they all "began to speak with other tongues, as the Spirit gave them utterance" (Ac 2:4). The inaugural coming of the Spirit and the constitution; of the Church were never to be repeated, but

---

[1] *Church of God Evangel*, Vol. 59, No.11 (May 19, 1959), pp 10-11.

the infilling of individuals with the accompanying sign is repeated several times after this in the accounts in Acts.

A multitude of Jews and proselytes, pilgrims from all parts of the world who had come to Jerusalem for the Feast of Pentecost, gathered as a result of the sound that they heard that day. They were bewildered and divided in opinion as to what was happening. Many were open enough to suggest that possibly this had some meaning of which they were not aware. But others mocked and said that these people had been drinking too early in the morning.

Then Peter, in the power of the Spirit, which Christ had said would make them witnesses (Ac 1:8), stood up, with the eleven, and explained the meaning of the event. He told them that God was fulfilling His promise to pour out His Spirit upon all flesh. Then Peter went on and said that Jesus who was crucified, had been raised from the dead and was now sitting at the right hand of God, and had received the promise of the Father and had poured out the Spirit. The same Holy Spirit who was working in Peter to give him the power to proclaim the message was also working in the hearts of the hearers. They were "cut to the heart," and, as a result, three thousand persons believed in Jesus and accepted him as their Lord.[2]

From this review of the happenings on the Day of Pentecost, we can see that the presence and power of the Holy Spirit is the dynamic of the Church. It is the Holy Spirit who makes the Church what it is, because it was He who fuses the believers together to constitute the Church. Any church today, if it is a

---

[2] In Peter's sermon on the Day of Pentecost, he answered the question, "What does this mean?' in two ways: (1) eschatologically, i.e., in terms of God's plan for the ages. God had promised that in the last days, when Messiah came, he would pour out his Spirit on all flesh, and this was happening before their eyes; and (2) christologically, i..e., in terms of Christ's work. The Messiah had come, he had died and he had risen---and as proof of his identity--had ascended to the right hand of the Father and, having received the promise of the Father, had poured out his Spirit, in order to form his body and to empower it to continue his work of redemption.

true manifestation of the Church invisible, is such only through the presence and power of the Holy Spirit. Otherwise, it is no more than a club. It is the Spirit who builds us "as lively stones...[into] a spiritual house" (1 Pe 2:5).

We live in a world of sin and darkness that is desperately in need of God. The hearts of the multitudes long for contact with their Creator; and many, all over the world, have turned from traditional ways of worship because they could not find the reality of the presence of God or fellowship with God. Worship was meaningless and empty; it was not sincere. But when a Christian experiences genuine spiritual communion with God, there is meaning, sincerity, and joy. This is the strength of Pentecostal worship. It is meaningful, sincere, and fervent because it brings people into contact with God, the ultimate spiritual reality.

The soul has a deep psychological need to belong, to be accepted, and to be united with other human beings. Complete fulfillment of this need is possible only when a person is in Christ and experiences, through the Holy Spirit, fellowship with Christ and others in his body.[3] It is this participation in Christ through the Holy Spirit that constitutes the body of Christ (1 Cor 12:12, 27) and in it, we are both parts of Christ and parts of each other, "members one of another" (Eph 4:25). In true Christian fellowship one experiences "the unity of the Spirit" (Eph 4:3).

This fellowship in the Spirit found various ways of expressing itself in the early church. They shared their material goods, especially with those in need, and ate their food together with glad and generous hearts, including the "breaking of the bread." The latter became a sacrament of their unity, a celebration of the presence of the Risen Christ in their midst, and a

---

[3] Fellowship is one translation of κοίνωνία (koi-no-NEE-ah) or participation in the Holy Spirit.

pledge to continue his ministry, as well as a memorial of His death.

Besides worship and fellowship, the event of Pentecost also brought to the Church an enduement of power for service. Evangelism was the inevitable result of this presence and power of the Holy Spirit in the Church. It was this power that changed Peter from the man who cringed at the scorn of the little door maid at the home of the high priest into the man who faced the whole Sanhedrin (the senate of Israel) and declared, "We must obey God rather than men."

The power of Pentecost has turned countless others, learned and unlearned, into staunch witnesses for Christ. Today so much of what is proclaimed from the pulpit fails to meet the needs of the people in the pew because it is not done in the power of the Holy Spirit. Many laymen of the church also prove ineffectual in their Christian life and witness for the same reason. We all have experienced what it means, to know of the good and not to be able to do it. The main purpose of the Holy Spirit is to give the believer the power to live for, and to serve, God and to witness to others.

The early Christians were commanded by the risen Christ to go into all the world and to preach the good news of salvation to every creature. It is the Holy Spirit who is the dynamic of this outreach. He, more than we, desires that Christ be preached and that all men repent and turn to God. It was the Holy Spirit who used Peter and drew three thousand persons to Christ on the Day of Pentecost, even before the Church had time to reflect on its purposes and activities. It was the Holy Spirit who guided Peter to preach to the first Gentiles and who spoke in the church at Antioch and said, "Set forth Barnabas and Saul for me unto the work to which I have called them" (Ac 13:3).

Wherever the Holy Spirit is given the proper place in the life of the church, there will be a harvest of souls. In Chile after the initial outpouring of the Holy Spirit in 1909, the Pentecostals, through the guidance of the Holy Spirit, took to the streets to preach and to witness to salvation in Christ. Literally hundreds of thousands were won and today nine out of every ten Protestants in Chile are Pentecostal.

The movement was even larger in Brazil as Spirit-filled laymen were moved to take Christ to the lost. In such movements in history we see the body of Christ continuing His work to seek and to save the lost. Through his body, empowered by his Holy Spirit, he continues to "build" his church (Mt 16:18). A vision, a compassion, and a ministry to win men and women to Christ will only come to a person by his surrendering all to Christ and yielding to the Holy Spirit.[4]

We can say with certainty that the Church---in its many dimensions of worship, fellowship, power for service, and evangelism---can only fulfill its function and purpose through the indwelling presence and power of the Holy Spirit. And against such a Church, clothed in this Pentecostal power, "the gates of hell shall not prevail" (Mt 16:18).

---

[4] See Luke 10:33-34. A man had been robbed and left half dead. When the Samaritan (1) saw him, (2) he had compassion on him and (3) ministered to him.

Alma Mater
Church of God Theological Seminary

Unto Thee, O God our Father,
  We now offer praise,
For Thy mercies in Christ Jesus
  In so many ways.
For our families and loved ones,
  And for colleagues too,
We now offer thanks unto Thee;
  Keep us always true.

From our hearts, O Lord, we thank Thee,
  For Thy love and grace;
Thy divine and holy calling
  Brought us to this place.
Here Thy Holy Spirit taught us,
  And our lives did mold;
Help us now to love and serve Thee,
  As the years unfold.

Bless, O Lord, our Alma Mater,
  May it always be,
Self-denying in Thy service,
  Loyal unto Thee.
May Thy Word and Holy Spirit
  Ever honored be;
In the teaching and the learning
  Glory be to Thee!   Amen!

Music: Traditional Melody based on Air: Annie Lisle
Written 3-10-92.

Part Four

The Mission of the Church

℘ ✿ ℆

TRUSTEES OF THE GOSPEL[1]

Put in trust with the gospel.
1 Th 2:4.

Paul was deeply conscious of the fact that he had been entrusted with the gospel. He wrote to Titus, "God ...has manifested his word through preaching, which is committed unto me according to the commandment of God our Savior" (Tit 1:2f). And, in almost the same words, he wrote to Timothy about "the glorious gospel of the blessed God, which was committed to my trust" (2 Tim 1:11). In our text, his first letter to the Thessalonians, he reminds them that "as we were allowed of God to be put in trust with the gospel, even so we speak." If the gospel is a trust, everyone who has received the gospel has, in a sense, become a trustee of the gospel. Everyone who has had the privilege of hearing the goodnews and has received the pardon that was purchased at Calvary has, by that very act, assumed an obligation to keep (guard, contend for) the faith and to pass it on.

What is a Trust?

In the legal world we have a modern-day parable of what Paul meant when he said that he was "put in trust" with the gospel. What I am speaking of is known as a "trust." Let us think about the different aspects of a trust. To begin let us look at a definition. A trust is *"an arrangement by which property is handed to or vested in a person, in the trust or confidence that he will use and dispose of it for the benefit of another.*[2]

---

[1] *Church of God Evangel* (Vol 47, No 38), Nov 26, 1956, p 6f.
[2] This and the following passages in italics are quoted from some source about trusts. At the time that this was written, I was in Haiti (1952-59), and since it was published as a motivational article, I failed to mention the

Persons Involved

Apart from the party making the trust, there are the following persons involved: The person who holds property in trust is a trustee; the person for whose benefit he holds it is called cestui que trust *(the one who has the benefit of the trust).*

In considering a trust we notice that there are three parties involved: (1) the party making the trust, (2) the party benefiting from the trust, and (3) the party administering the trust. With this in mind let us consider the gospel. Are these three parties involved in the trust of the gospel? Yes! "For God so loved the world that He gave His only begotten Son so that whosoever believes...(but) how can they believe in Him of whom they have not heard? and how shall they hear without a preacher?" (Jn 3:16; Rom 10:14). (1) God, our heavenly Father, is the party making the trust, (2) the world (whosoever) is the party benefiting from the trust, and (3) the messenger, the proclaimer of the good news, is the party administering the trust. The messenger in this sense is not necessarily a minister as opposed to a layman. In Ac 8:4, we read, "Therefore they that were scattered abroad went everywhere preaching the word." In this case it was the members of the church, not the apostles, who were scattered and preached.[3]

I. The Party Making the Trust

As far as the law is concerned, anyone (theoretically) can make a trust, but there are two practical considerations: **First**, one must have the necessary disposition; **second**, one must have the means. Without the necessary disposition no trust was ever established, whether for the benefit of some friend or relative, or for the furtherance of some great cause, such as the great philanthropic foundations or trusts for medical, educa-

---

source that I was quoting. Now after nearly fifty years, I cannot determine what that source was.

[3] A scholar once said that the gospel was gossiped across the Roman empire. In other words it was transmitted from person to person.

tional and scientific purposes. Included in that disposition is the vision of a need, a compassionate affection toward the person or persons suffering that need, and a willingness to act.

Our heavenly Father had such a disposition toward a wayward and sinful humanity. He "so loved" the world that He gave heaven's best that we might become a partaker of the divine nature and drink of the fountain of eternal life. We can talk about our need and read what the Bible has to say about it, but the human mind can never grasp, as the Infinite did, the utter lostness, ruin and degradation that we suffer. What should move Him to tenderness, affection and love toward a rebellious, ungodly, wicked race is the mystery and secret of infinite love. As the poet asked, "Why should He love me so?"[4]

Then, too, the terrible condition caused by sin required a tremendous price for the purchase of our salvation. Neither among men nor angels was such a price to be found. No sacrifice but God's sacrifice was sufficient. "For it is not possible that the blood of bulls and of goats should take away sins" (Heb 10:4). "You were not redeemed with corruptible things, as silver and gold,...but with the precious blood of Christ" (1 Pet 1:18f). So, God gave His only begotten Son, heaven's Jewel, as the price of our redemption. He died in our stead that we might live in Him. He who was rich became poor, that we, through His poverty, might become rich. He is the Way, the only Way, the ladder from earth to heaven.[5] "There is none other name under heaven given among men, whereby we must be saved" (Ac 4:12). Thank God for that wonderful name!

Not only was God willing, and not only did he have the means to establish a trust, but He did, in fact, establish such a trust. And it was He who designated the beneficiaries of that trust and the rules under which they could become partakers.

---

[4] Robert Harkness, "Why Should He Love Me So?" © copyright 1925. Renewed 1952 by Broadman Press.
[5] Cf. Jn 1:51 and Gen 28:12.

And it was also He who established the trustees and the rules governing their administration.

II. The Party Benefiting From the Trust

A trust always designates the *cestui que trust*, and so does the gospel.

> My little children, these things write I unto you, that ye sin not. And if any man sin, we have an advocate with the Father, Jesus Christ the righteous: And he is the propitiation for our sin: and not for ours only, but also for the sins of the whole world" (1 Jn 2:1f).

The whole world! "For God so loved the world ..." The whole world! "It is not the will of the Father that any should perish" (2 Pet 3:9). No, not a single one! Whosoever will may come.

Let us look at a tuberculosis foundation and hospital as an illustration. It states simply that anyone, regardless of race, color or creed, may receive treatment---anyone suffering from tuberculosis. That is how it is with the gospel. As when Moses lifted the brazen serpent on high, whosoever will may look and live. There is a standing invitation, "Come unto me" (Mt 11:28).

What, then, are the conditions for becoming a partaker and a beneficiary of this trust? We have the answer in the first recorded message of Jesus, "Repent, and believe the gospel" (Mk 1:15)---repentance and faith, turning from sin and turning to God, leaving Egypt and entering Canaan---forsaking sin and accepting Christ. Yes, "the gospel...is the power of God unto salvation to every one who believes" (Rom 1:16). But "how shall they believe in him of whom they have not heard?...Faith comes by hearing, and hearing by the word of God" (Rom 10:14,17). This is why God made every Christian a trustee of the gospel.

III. The Party Administering the Trust

Qualifications: The trustees of the gospel are chosen and approved of God. God called the prophets, and Christ called the apostles. Every Christian, every minister and every layman, is called of God. The Church, as a whole, is God's chosen company of trustees of the gospel. Certain qualifications are required in the trustees in order that they may be approved of God.

First, they must be in Christ and hold to the truth themselves. And they must be willing to tell what the Lord has done for them and what he can do for others.[6]

Second, they must live in accordance with the truth, "nor of uncleanness" (1 Th 2:3). The trustee of the holy gospel must be a regenerate person, who lets Christ rule and reign within. Otherwise, his conduct will annul the message that he speaks.

Third, they must be honest in the discharge of the trust, "nor in guile (duplicity)" (1 Th 2:3) There should be no self-seeking, no double-dealing, and no men-pleasing in the presentation of the gospel. They must be sincerely devoted to the truth that is entrusted to them.

Duties: *The main duties of trustees are (1) to place the trust property in a proper state of security, (2) to keep it (if personal), in safe custody, and (3) properly invest and distribute it. A trustee must be careful not to place himself in a position where his interest might clash with his duty.*

1. Duties Related to the Trust Property

Let us look at the paragraph on the duties of the trustee again. This time let us examine it in three parts. *The main duties of trustees are to place the trust property in a proper state of se-*

---

[6] Cf. Mk 5:19.

curity, to keep it in safe custody. First of all, the trustee of the gospel is a guardian of the gospel. He should endeavor to keep it pure and holy and unchanged. He has no right to add to or subtract from the gospel. As Paul said, "The Gospel which I preached unto you" is "received" and "according to the Scriptures" (1 Cor 15:1-3). Trustees should "earnestly contend for the faith which was once (for all) delivered unto the saints" (Jude 3). They are custodians of the full gospel.

The statement of duties continues thus: *and properly invest and distribute it.* The framers of this document had in mind what we learn from the parables of the talent and the sower. So the trustees of the gospel are not only guardians and custodians but also investors and distributors of the gospel.[7] They are to invest the talents that the Lord has given them and sow the gospel seed. The gospel is of such a nature that it is natural for those who respond to it to tell others about it (Jn 1:40f).

Now the final sentence from this statement of duties is this:. *A trustee must be careful not to place himself in a position where his interest might clash with his duty.* In other words, trustees should be careful to avoid getting themselves in a place where what they want to do would conflict with what they should do. There is an obligation upon everyone who has become a partaker of the gospel to send it forth into all the world. Paul felt that way concerning himself and said, "Woe to me, if I do not preach the gospel" (1 Cor 9:16)! However, at the same time he realized that the reward only comes from being willing. "For if I do this willingly, I have a reward" (1 Cor 9:17). May we ever be delivered from the evil one who continually tries to make us put what we think is our own self-interest in opposition to our service to God. We must be willing trustees of the gospel.

---

[7] Cf. Paul's designation of ministers, "Stewards of the mysteries of God" (1 Cor 4:1).

2. Duties Related to the Other Parties

We have already considered some of the duties of the trustee as relating to the trust property. Now let us look at some of the duties and relationships of the trustee as relating to the other parties involved in the trust. In a way, the trustee stands between the party making the trust and the party benefiting from the trust. And in that sense he is a representative of both. Every Christian is an "ambassador for Christ," and, as such, is God's royal representative. Paul uses a twofold illustration to explain our representation.

> Now then we are ambassadors for Christ, (1) as though God did beseech you by us (here God is the active agent; we are the instruments): (2) we pray you in Christ's stead (here we are the active personal agents, but acting in the name of and representing Christ), 'Be ye reconciled to God' (2 Cor 5:20).

We are the instruments and representatives of God declaring the word of reconciliation to the world. And in this capacity, it is very necessary to have the mind of Christ (Phil 2:5). And His mind was to lay aside all prerogative and to commit himself to the ministry of redemption. He was concerned for the lost and pressed onward to go "into the next towns" (Mk 1:38) with the word of life. Before He ascended, He made His will plain. After saying, "All authority is given unto me in heaven and on earth," he said "Go into all the world, and preach the gospel to every creature" (Mk 16:15). All the power of heaven and earth is behind us.

Since the trustee is a representative of the two parties, he is responsible to both. First, the representative of the gospel is responsible to God.

> For the kingdom of heaven is as a man traveling into a far country, who called his own servants, and delivered unto them his goods...After a long time the lord of those servants came, and reckoned with them" (Mt 25:14,19).

Yes, our Lord is coming and there is a reckoning day ahead. We are answerable for that which He has committed into our hands. "Moreover it is required in stewards, that they be found faithful" (1 Cor 4:2).

And second, the trustee is also the representative of the beneficiary of the trust, which in this case is "whosoever will." The welfare and rightful dues of the beneficiary should be uppermost in the mind of the trustee. So trustees of the gospel are not only royal representatives of God but also a "royal priesthood" (1 Pet 2:9) to make intercession "for all men" (1 Tim 2:1). Too often, prayer is looked upon as a secret weapon or a guided missile---to be used only in dire necessity, and rarely. We need to take it out of the classified files and put it to work for the evangelization of the world. Yes, it is a guided missile and very effective, but it must be put to use in order to get results.

Thus the trustee is responsible to the beneficiary; and this creates an obligation. It is clear that we, as Christians, are obligated and, therefore, responsible to God. It is not so often realized that we are obligated and, therefore, bear a responsibility to the lost and dying around the world, also. Paul said, "I am debtor both to the Greeks, and to the Barbarians; both to the wise, and to the unwise. So, as much as in me is, I am ready to preach the gospel..." (Rom 1:14f). We might ask, "Paul, you do mean that you owe it to the heathen to take them the gospel? Do you not mean that you owe it to God to take them the gospel? Do you not mean that you are doing the heathen a favor to take them the gospel?" I hear him, who bore about in his body the dying of the Lord Jesus, answer, "No, I understand my debt to God, but I also understand my debt to the heathen. The gospel that I received was given to me to be given to others. I owe it to others to give them the gospel."[8] Every trustee of the gospel is a debtor.

A Sevenfold Comparison
Between a Trustee of the Gospel and a Legal Trustee

Following are seven statements which throw light on the office of a legal trustee. With each there is a seed thought for the trustee of the gospel.

1. *A trustee's is not a compulsory office, but gratuitous; but if he once accepts he is not at liberty afterward to renounce, unless the trust deed contain a provision enabling him to do so, or the court for good reasons discharge him.* No one is forced to, but anyone can, by the grace of God, become a trustee of the gospel. A Christian is not at liberty to renounce his trusteeship of the gospel unless he renounce the blessings of the gospel as well. But there is such a thing as discharge for disqualification.

2. *A trustee cannot delegate the office to a third person, but continues personally bound to his duty.* As Christians we must not think that we can pay the preacher---whether pastor, evangelist or missionary---and then be relieved of our duty. No, we are personally bound to our trusteeship; it cannot be delegated to another.

3. *Where there are several trustees appointed, the office is considered joint, so that if one dies, the survivors continue to exercise the office.* We are not alone in our trusteeship of the gospel; "God buries His workers, but His work goes on."[9]

---

[8] For a long time I did not understand how Paul was a debtor to the lost. Then it came to me; he was the postman and he had letters addressed to the lost and therefore he owed it to the lost to get the message to them.

[9] Exact source unknown, but attributed by some to John Wesley.

4. *As a rule, all must join in doing any act; but if the trust is of a public nature, a majority may bind the minority.*
Each of us is a part of the body of Christ and is exhorted to have the mind of Christ. Therefore all of us, united by the Spirit and by love, should be committed to sending forth the gospel.

5. *Each trustee is liable only for his own acts or defaults.*
Each trustee of the gospel is personally accountable for the discharge of his trusteeship. He does not have to answer for anybody else on the reckoning day.

6. *Another rule is that a trustee is not allowed to make a gain of his office (this has certain exceptions).* "Freely ye have received, freely give" (Mt 10:8). The exception, "The Lord ordained that those who preach the gospel should live of the gospel" (1 Cor 9:14).

7. *As a rule, trustees must pay interest whether they invest the funds or not (if they have had time to invest) to the* **cestui que trust**. "You wicked and slothful servant, you knew that I reap where I have not sown, and gather where I have not scattered; therefore you ought to have invested my money, and then at my coming I should have received what I gave you, plus interest" (Mt 25:26f).

It is a glorious and fearful thing that the Almighty has entrusted us, the church, with the awesome task of proclaiming the gospel to every creature. Let us be faithful to that trust. ✤

ဆ ⚜ ﬤ

A MISSION-MINDED CHURCH[1]

Let this mind be in you, which was also in Christ Jesus.
Phil 2:5

"Mission-Minded" is a phrase that should be heard more often today. It is the desire of those who know the needs of our Church and our world that our churches and our members be involved in the world mission of the Church. By that we mean, disposed and inclined to missions or having an interest in, a love for, and an active participation in missions. And by missions we mean, the sending forth of the gospel into all the world, from "Jerusalem... unto the uttermost part of the earth," from center to circumference.

If we seek a Biblical content for our phrase "Mission-minded," I think that we find it in our text: "Let this mind be in you, which was also in Christ Jesus." The text refers to the whole scope of Christian living in general, but when applied to missions, we can say that to be missions-minded means to have the mind of Christ concerning the sending forth of the gospel into all the world.

There is one interesting thing to notice about our text. The word *mind* in the original is a verb and not a noun--thus indicating action and not naming an object. Paul uses the same verb in his letter to the Romans (8:5), "For they that are after the flesh do mind the things of the flesh; but they that are after the Spirit the things of the Spirit." *Pulpit Commentary* throws some light on this verse in its commentary on Philippians 2:5.[2]

---

[1] *Church of God Evangel*, (Vol 48, No 25) August 26, 1957, pp. 4f
[2] B. C. Caffin, *Philippians*, p. 59, in H. D. M. Spence and Joseph S. Exell, *The Pulpit Commentary* (Grand Rapids: Wm. B. Eerdmans, reprint 1950).

Caffin proposed to translate it this way: "Mind this in you which was also (minded) in Christ Jesus." Or we could say, "Be concerned about what Christ is concerned about."

> The words, 'in Christ Jesus,' show that the corresponding words, 'in you,' cannot mean 'among you,' but 'in your-selves,' 'in your heart.' ... He bids us mind (compare Romans viii.8) the things which the Lord Jesus minded, to love what he loved, to hate what he hated; the thoughts; desires, motives, of the Christian should be the thoughts, desires, motives which filled the sacred heart of Jesus Christ our Lord.[3]

So in the light of this, let us turn to the Gospels to find what the mind of Christ was, and is, as touching missions, i.e., what He "minded" concerning the sending forth of the gospel. Then let us see how it applies to the church, as illustrated in Paul, the church's greatest missionary, and as the message of God to us today.

The Story That Shows the Secret

One day Jesus told a story that we have come to call "The Good Samaritan" (Lk 10:25-37). "A certain man went down from Jerusalem to Jericho, and fell among thieves, who stripped him of his raiment, and wounded him, and departed, leaving him half dead." What a picture of the highway of life and a wounded world! There are multitudes today who have been overpowered by the enemy of their souls, stripped and wounded, and left dying---wrecks on the highway of life.

> And by chance there came down a certain priest that way: and when he saw him, he passed by on the other side. And likewise a Levite, when he was at the place, came and looked on him, and passed by on the other side.

Here we see religious indifference, the high and holy of the world who pass by with no pity or compassion and who are not touched or concerned with the lost and dying.

---

[3] *Ibid.*

But a certain Samaritan, as he journeyed, came to where he was: and when he saw him, he had compassion on him, and went to him, and bound up his wounds, pouring in oil and wine, and set him on his own beast, and brought him, to an inn, and took care of him. And on the following day when he left, he took out two pence, and gave them to the host, and said unto him, Take care of him; and whatever you spend, more than this, when I come again, I will repay you. (Lk 10:33-35)

Here we have the mind and disposition of the Master!

One of my Bible professors once said that this story shows us three attitudes toward life---that of the robbers: what is yours is mine and I will take it; that of the priest and Levite: what is mine is mine and I will keep it; and that of the Samaritan: what is mine is yours and I will share it.

Now let us take a closer look at this Samaritan who "as he journeyed, came where he (the wounded man) was." That speaks to my mind of opportunity. This man was going down that winding descent to Jericho. He did not know what lay ahead, but he rounded a curve, and there before him, as though flung in his path, was opportunity. As travelers on the road of life, how true we know this to be. It is equally true of our Church. We have "journeyed" a long way, and we have come to a place of opportunity such as we have never known before.

Then the Master gave us the secret. "When he saw him, he had compassion on him, and ...(ministered) to him." We can sum it up in three words: vision, compassion, and ministry. We could state it in three verbs: look, love, and lift. We could illustrate it in three word-pictures: open our eyes to see, open our heart to care, and open our hands to help.

Vision

Jesus had a vision! He saw us, his human creatures, robbed of the glory of God and dying by the highway of life. He saw us blinded and chained in the prison house of sin. "When (Jesus) saw the multitudes, he was moved with compassion on them, because they fainted, and were scattered abroad, as sheep having no shepherd" (Mt 9:36). He saw them as a great harvest field, the grain bowing down, the storm coming, and the harvest in danger.

Jesus had had a mighty ministry in Capernaum. One morning, rising up a great while before day, he went into a solitary place, and there prayed. And Simon and they that were with him followed after him. And when they had found him, they said unto him, All men seek for thee.

What a temptation this would be to us today! It meant success and the applause of the multitudes! But none of these things moved Him. Instead, He said unto His disciples, "Let us go on to the next towns, that I may preach there also: because this is why I came" (Mk 1:38). He had a vision of why He had come.

Paul, too, had a vision (Rom 15:20f).

And this is why I have endeavored to preach the gospel, not where Christ was named, lest I should build on someone else's foundation: But as it is written,
Those who had not been informed shall see;
and those who had not heard shall understand.

In another place he speaks of the "regions beyond" (2 Cor 10:16). He had a vision of reaching out, both as touching the need of those who had not yet heard and as touching the necessity laid on him to preach the gospel.

The Church should have a vision, a twofold vision, a vision of the field and a vision of God's Word. The Master is still speaking to His Church in the words addressed to His disciples so long ago: "Lift up your eyes, and look on the fields; for they are white and ready for harvest" (Jn 4:35). Look until physical things fade away and you can see the souls of men and women, lost without God and without a hope in the world. Look until you can see the life-smothering clutch of sin, its death-dealing strangle-hold on all who have not received the Lord.. Look until you can see millions of your fellow human beings bowing down to some grotesque image of the Buddha. Look until you see other millions prostrating themselves toward Mecca five times a day, every day that rolls over our heads, to proclaim: "There is no god but Allah, and Mohammed is his prophet." Look until you can see the hundreds of millions caught in the deception of the great deceiver: millions of simple, "primitive and uncivilized" people who openly worship demons and devils, and millions of "civilized and cultured" people caught in the snare of every "ism" in the dictionary. May we look until we have a vision of the field, remembering that "the field is the world."

As a second part of our vision and to complete it, we need to behold the Word of God until we see the power of the gospel, God's great purpose for mankind, and our place in God's plan. We need to know with Paul that "the gospel of Christ....is the power of God unto salvation to every one who believes" (Rom 1:16). It is not a myth or a theory, but the unshackling, delivering, life-giving power of God. We need to let these words of our resurrected Savior ring in our ears over and over again "Go into all the world and preach the gospel to every creature" (Mk 16:15). Do you still have an alibi? Then you have not listened long enough. Are you still putting it off on somebody else? Then you have not listened long enough. Listen again. "But you shall receive power, when the Holy Spirit is come upon you; and you shall be my witnesses, both in Jerusalem, and in all Judea, and in Samaria, and unto the uttermost part of the earth" (Ac 1:8). That is His purpose, and our part is sending forth the Word of Life.

Compassion

Jesus was moved with compassion when He saw the suffering and sinfulness of the people around him.. When a leper (Mk 1:40f) came kneeling and saying, "If you will, you can make me clean," this is what we read: "And Jesus, moved with compassion, put forth his hand, and touched him, and said to him, I will; be clean." After a busy and active ministry, Jesus, with full knowledge of the supreme sacrifice which lay ahead, journeyed toward Jerusalem, the beloved city. "And when he had come near, he beheld the city, and wept over it, saying, 'If you, even you, this day only knew, the things that lead to peace! But they are now hidden from your eyes" (Lk 19:41f). Oh! boundless compassion of a tender Saviour!

Paul, too, knew that compassion which is the mainspring of service. He said, "For the love of Christ constrains us" (2 Cor 5:14). What kept you going, Paul, when you were rejected, stoned, beaten, shipwrecked, and suffered a multitude of other insults and brutalities? What was it, Paul? And he would surely say, "The constraining love of the Matchless One who met me that day on the road to Damascus, him, whose I am and whom I serve." That is why he could write the Corinthians, "And I will very gladly spend and be spent for you" (2 Cor 12:15). That is also why Paul wrote concerning Israel,

> I have great heaviness and continual sorrow in my heart. For I could wish that myself were accursed from Christ for my brethren, my kinsmen according to the flesh ...my heart's desire and prayer to God for Israel is, that they might be saved" (Rom 9:2f; 10:1).

The Church must have that compassion, too. Jesus said that it was easy to love those who love you, but He desires us to love the unlovely and the unloving. Jesus spoke to *us* when he told the lawyer, "Go, and do thou likewise" (Lk 10:37), i.e., show compassion on the unfortunate, mistreated, and suffering. "But not on this despised foreigner?" "Yes, even on him." Love is a mighty thing. You can love more people into the kingdom of God than you can get in by persuasion, psychology, argument, or anything else. There is a little verse which goes as follows:

> *Lord, lay some soul upon my heart,*
> *And love that soul through me;*

And may I always do my part
To win that soul for Thee.[4]

There are some interesting things about love. The more we love, the more love we have, both within and from others. Sending forth our love does not impoverish us. The more we export, the more we have at home. Love puts us in tune with the nature of things. All discord and strife dissolve before it. Unkind words and acts have to go. Selfishness cannot stand before outgoing love (cf. 1 Cor 13). Love seeks expression. It seeks to manifest itself in action. That brings us to our next consideration.

Ministry

We have seen that there are three component parts or con-secutive steps in Christian service: vision, compassion and ministry (action and service). Some persons take one; some, two; and some, all three of these steps. Many take the first step because of circumstances. The priest and the Levite did this. They caught a glimpse of a need and hurried along their own selfish way. There are others who, having seen the need, pour out a certain semblance of compassion but go no farther. Those are the sentimentalists. But, thank God, there are others, like this "certain Samaritan," who are willing to get involved and serve.

In the gospels we see that Jesus' vision and compassion issued in a life of service and ministry... "Jesus went about all the cities and villages, teaching ... and preaching....and healing...." (Mt 9:35). Peter spoke of "how God anointed Jesus of Nazareth with the Holy Spirit and with power: who went about doing good, and healing all who were oppressed of the devil; for God was with him" (Ac 10:38). The life of Christ is an

---

[4] By Baylus Benjamin McKinney in collaboration with Mack Weaver; first printed in the Broadman Hymnal (Nashville: Broadman Press, 1940).

illustration of His idea of true greatness, which He explained in terms of service.

Paul was another whose life issued in service. Paul could sum up his ministry thus:

> For I will not dare to speak of any of those things which Christ hath not wrought by me, to make the Gentiles obedient, by word and deed, through mighty signs and wonders, by the power of the Spirit of God; so that from Jerusalem, and round about to Illyricum, I have fully preached the gospel of Christ (Rom 15:18f).[5]

"Fully preached"---what a full life was his---full of service and ministry!

The ministry of the local church finds an apt illustration in two things: the radiation of light and the outreaching hand. When Jesus said, "Let your light so shine before men" (Mt 5:16), he was not speaking just to the ministry and to the missionaries. He was speaking to every individual Christian. The ministry of the local church---its influences, its witness, its words, its actions, its prayers, its giving---all of these radiate as light into the darkness.

Several years ago World Missions put out a film, entitled "Hands Across the Caribbean." Where could we find a more appropriate illustration of the ministry of the local church than outreaching hands, reaching across the sea and around the world?

In what does this ministry of the local church as concerning missions consist? We might sum it up in three words: praying, witnessing, and giving. These are the three frequencies, or channels, to borrow a figure of speech from radio and television, on which the local church can broadcast to the whole world. But how often our voltage is so low that we do not reach very far. And alas! most of us do not have directional antennas.

---

[5] A paraphrase of this would be something like this: "You wouldn't believe all that Christ has done through me to make the Gentiles obedient..."

Prayer has been called, and truly is, the mightiest force in the world. We know that, but how often our prayers are confined to a small radius because of our lack of vision. We say, "But I'm not acquainted with any particular field. How can I know how to pray for it?" The needs and problems are those of the Church in general, and you can pray for such things as the following: the need for missionaries and national workers, the problem of training ministers of the Gospel, the need for revival with the mighty convicting power of the Holy Spirit, the need of new converts and babes in Christ to grow in grace and the knowledge of our Lord and Savior, Jesus Christ, and to be equipped to be an active part of the body and mission of Jesus Christ, the need for a mighty outpouring of the Holy Spirit on Christians in general, the need for doors to be opened and barriers broken down, the need for buildings, the need for literature, and many other things both spiritual and material. Yes, the local church needs a mighty, outreaching ministry of intercession which will literally girdle the globe. You have heard story after story of how somebody prayed and how God answered halfway around the world. It means much to a missionary to know that he or she is being held up in prayer. They are out on the frontier between light and darkness. We, the Church, sent them out there. Let us not let them down when it comes to prayer. The task is not just one person's ministry; it is the ministry of the whole church. Let us pray!

Every local church should bear a vital, energetic witness to the gospel. If we hold the torch high enough and proudly enough, our young people will catch the gleam and the challenge. As they go forth, some as Sunday school and church workers, some as ministers here at home, and some as missionaries in all parts of the world, the ministry of the local church goes out through their witnessing. Every missionary goes out from some local church. In a very real way, he is the extension of the ministry of that local church. There will be a reward for those who won him to Christ and inspired him to Christian service. Let us witness!

The third aspect of this missionary ministry of the local church could be called the ministry of giving. Giving is as much a ministry as anything else we do. Let us take a short lesson in economics to see if we can throw some light on giving. A person works for an employer for a week, which means that this person has taken so much time and so much energy and used them performing some service for the employer. As payment, he receives money. What are those bills? Considered from the point of view of inherent value, they are practically worthless. Their value lies in what they represent. In economics, money is called a "medium of exchange." That is exactly what our money is. It represents so many hours or days of our life at our work. Its value is in the fact that we can buy groceries and clothes, pay house rent, buy a house, send our children to school, etc., with this money. So when we pay our tithes and give offerings, we are giving so many hours and days out of our lives for the Lord and His work. When we give for world missions, we are saying, "I cannot go myself, but I am sending so many days out of my life, spent here at my work at home, across the seas and around the world to support some missionary and carry on God's work." When we understand our giving in this light, then we understand how our missionary giving is an outreaching, vital part of the ministry of the local church. Let us give!

Paul wrote to the Philippians, "Let this mind be in you, which was also in Christ Jesus" (2:5). If the local church has the mind of Christ, surely it will catch something of that vision that inspired Him, something of that compassion that filled His heart, and something of that ministry that occupied all His energies. Lord, give us open eyes to see, open hearts to care, and open hands to serve! ✤

၈ဩ ✾ ငၩ

THE GREAT COMMISSION *

Go ye therefore,
and teach (make disciples of) all nations,
baptizing them in the name of the Father,
and of the Son, and of the Holy Spirit,
teaching them to observe all things
that I have commanded you.
Mt 28:19f

When we hear the words "the great commission," we probably recall the words of our Lord as recorded by Matthew
above. We have come to call this the Great Commission.
And, at the same time, we may also think, "Thank God for the
missionaries who do that." But the great commission is not
addressed just to missionaries; it is directed to the whole
church. The words of Jesus are spoken to us---the church as a
whole and each of us individually. "Just as the Father sent me,
I also am sending you" (Jn 20:21). Therefore, it is our task to
go or to send, and if we send, it is our task to pray and to give.

Let us think of the great commission in the light of the two
great commandments, the first of which is "Love the Lord your
God with all your heart, with all your soul, with all your mind,
and with all your strength" (Mk 12:30). God loved us and
gave us a Savior, who made it possible for us to be forgiven
and to have everlasting life (Jn 3:16). God still loves the
world; and it is not the will of God that any should perish, but
that all should come to repentance (2 Pet 3:9). Jesus said, "If

---

* The original of this chapter was first written as a tract for Westmore
Church of God, Cleveland, Tennessee.

you love me, you will keep my commandments" (Jn 14:15). If
we really love God, will we not be eager to do His will, and,
especially, to have a part in His work of redemption?

The second commandment is "Love your neighbor as yourself" (Mk 12:31). The neighbor is the one, in whatever circumstances, to whom we have an opportunity to do good (Lk
10:25-37). And that person is also the one "for whom Christ
died" (1 Cor 8:12). If God cares so much, how can it be of no
importance to me?

Let us also think of the great commission in the light of the
Lord's Prayer (Mt 6:9-13), which, one would suppose, was in-
tended for daily use. It is, clearly, a prayer for the believer because it is addressed to "our Father...in heaven." And by confessing God as our Father, we put ourselves among His children and acknowledge that we are part of his family (1 Jn 3:1).
What a privilege! A child of the heavenly Father!

The first three petitions of the Lord's Prayer are related to
God's will and work in the world---the purposes of the Father.
(1) "Hallowed be thy name" or "May your name be honored as
holy." This, in one sense, is a prayer for the salvation of the
lost, for how can others honor His name as holy unless they
hear the good-news and come to trust in Jesus Christ as Savior
and Lord? (2) "Thy kingdom come" or "May you be recognized as King! May your kingship be extended." Yes, the
King is coming! And He shall reign! But, in the meantime,
the kingdom is being extended from heart to heart. The Word
grows and the Kingdom is coming to multiplied thousands (Ac
6:7; 12:24; 19:20). And, wonder of wonders, we have the
wonderful privilege of being part of it! (3) "Thy will be done
on earth as it is in heaven." As the kingdom expands, more
people are made new creatures, their minds are renewed, and
they begin to do the will of God. O what a privilege of having
such a heavenly Father and being an instrument in his holy
hands!

In the second half of the Lord's Prayer, we pray for things that focus more on ourselves, but not just on ourselves. (1) "Give us this day our daily bread" or "Give us this day the bread that we need." We are finite and dependent creatures. We must receive day by day that which renews our strength, i.e., both the natural bread and the bread from heaven. The hungry multitudes are all around us. Jesus breaks the Bread of Life and gives it to us to share with the hungry. We, therefore, owe it both to Him and to them to give out the Bread of Life. (2) "Forgive us our trespasses as we forgive those who trespass against us," or "Forgive us where we have failed, as we have forgiven those who have failed us." With all our best intentions we fail, but there is forgiveness if the heart is open in forgiveness to others. And to think of all those who have never known the transforming power of the grace and forgiveness of God in the first place! "Father, forgive them, for they know not what they do" (Lk 23:34)! (3) "Lead us not into temptation, but deliver us from evil" Evil and the evil one lie in wait for us, and indeed they beset every human being. As a race we have fallen into sin and are dominated by the evil one (1 Jn 5:19b). But there is redemption! The price has been paid (1 Pet 1:18f), and we have been freed! Yet behold how many there are still in bondage in the prison-house of sin.

But thank God, who sent his Son; and he said,

> The Spirit of the Lord is upon me
> > because He has anointed me
> > > to preach the gospel to the poor;
> > He has sent me
> > > to heal the brokenhearted
> > > to preach deliverance to the captive
> > > > and the recovery of sight to the blind,
> > > to preach the acceptable year of the Lord   **Lk 4:18f**

Jesus quoted this passage from Isaiah (61:1-2a) concerning his ministry while in the flesh. Now we are in Christ, the Anointed, so that he may continue his ministry through us.

The doxology of the Lord's Prayer, i.e., "For the Kingdom (sovereignty), the power and the glory are yours for ever and ever. Amen," reminds us that God is God and God is able. He will come, and He will reign! (Rev 11:15). But millions are lost---in darkness and in sin. The harvest is great, but the laborers are few. What shall we do? "Pray to the Lord of the Harvest that He will send forth laborers into the Harvest" (Mt 9:38).

Lord, what is my part in the end-time harvest? Help me and your people everywhere to hear your voice, to see the opportunity that you have placed before us and to be obedient to the heavenly calling. Help us to arise and give ourselves to the task, in the name of Jesus and in the power of the Spirit, that all may know.

My Involvement In the Mission of God

(1) When he saw him, (2) he had compassion on him, (3) and went to him, and bound up his wounds. *Jesus* (Luke 10:33f)

❖ **Vision:** *When he saw him...*
Help me, O Lord, to "lift up (my) eyes and look on the fields" and to understand your will and mission for your church in the world (Jn 4:35).

❖ **Compassion:** *He had compassion on him...*
May I, O Lord, be "moved with (the) compassion" that moved your heart as you looked on the multitudes, "because they were like sheep without a shepherd" (Mt 9:36).

❖ **Ministry:** *And went to him and bound up his wounds...*
And may I, O Lord, remember "whose I am and whom I serve" and be willing to participate in your mission in the world in every way that I can (Ac 27:23). ❖

Indices

Scripture References

Subject Index

Subjects in
The Teachings Made Prominent
See also pp 9-11.

1. Repentance, 6, 10, 14, 16, 19, 122, 149.
2. Justification, 7, 14f.
3. Regeneration or New Birth, 8, 10, 14f, 22, 72f, 75, 131..
5. Sanctification subsequent to Justification, 8, 10, 13, 15f, 69-77.
   * Sanctification (definition) 23, 71f.
   * Sanctification and Holiness 10, 15f, 103.
   * New birth vs sanctification, 73f.
   * Purity vs maturity, 75f.
   * Humanity vs carnality, 74f.
   * In the Flesh, in the Spirit, 48.
   * Perfection, 76f.
6. Holiness, 10, 13, 15, 75ff, 103.
7. Water Baptism, 6f, 10, 13, 16-18, 21f, 91f, 149.
8. Baptism in the Holy Spirit subsequent to cleansing: the enduement of power for service, 6-10, 13f, 16f, 21-26, 35f, 52, 119-123.
9. The Speaking in Tongues as the Spirit gives utterance as the initial evidence of the baptism of the Holy Ghost, 10, 17, 21, 36-39, 45f, 119.
10. Spiritual Gifts, 10, 17f, 27-49, 42, 49.

11. Signs following believers, 10, 17, 25f, 36, 41f, 110 , 11f.
12. Fruit of the Spirit, 10, 17, 42, 46, 49, 79f.
13. Divine Healing provided for all in the atonement, 10, 18, 144, 151.
    * Gift(s) of Healing(s) 43f.
14. The Lord's Supper, 10, 18.
15. Washing the saints' feet, 10, 18.
16. Tithing and Giving.
17. Restitution where possible, 11, 18f.
18. Premillennial second coming of Jesus.
    First, to resurrect the dead saint and to catch away the living saints to Him in the air. **Second**, to reign on the earth a thousand years.
19. Resurrection, 7, 11f, 113-117.
20. Eternal life for the righteous, 6f, 11, 15, 19, 129, 133, 149..
21. Eternal punishment for the wicked: No liberation nor annihilation, 11, 19.
22. Total abstinence from all liquor or strong drinks.
23. Against the use of tobacco in any form, opium, morphine, etc.
24. Meats and drinks, 97.
25. The Sabbath, 11, 20.

Authors Cited[1]

Barth, Karl, *Credo* (New York: Charles Scribner's sons, 1936) and *Bosquejo de Dogmática (Outline of Dogmatics)*, tr. by M. Guiterrez-Marin (Buenos Aires: La Aurora, 1954).

Bauer, Walter, William F. Arndt and F. Wilbur Gringich, *A Greek-English Lexicon of the New Testament and other early Christian literature* (Chicago: University of Chicago Press, 1957).

Buber, Martin, *Two Types of Faith* (New York: Harper and Row, 1961).

Caffin, B. C., *Philippians* in *Pulpit Commentary* (Grand Rapids: Wm. B. Eerdmans, 1950).

Conzelmann, Hans, *I Corinthians* (Philadelphia: Fortress, 1975).

Demant, V.A., *Christian Sex Ethics* (New York: Harper and Row, 1963).

Deren, Maya, *Divine Horsemen, Voodoo Gods of Haiti* (New York: Chelsea House, 1970).

Dodd, C. H. *The Apostolic Preaching, Three Lectures* (New York: Harper and Brothers, 1944) and *Gospel and Law* (New York: Columbia University Press, 1951).

Hiltner, Seward, *Sex and the Christian Life*, New York: Association Press, 1957.

Lewis, C. S., *Mere Christianity,* London: Geoffrey Bles, 1953.

Rackham, Richard, *The Acts of the Apostles* (London: Methuen, 1957).

Richardson, Alan, *a Theological Word Book of the Bible ???* *p63, 67*

Sisk, Leonard W., *Entire Sanctification* (Published Privately).

Thielicke, Helmut, *The Ethics of Sex,* New York: Harper and Row, 1964.

Vine, W. E., *A Comprehensive Dictionary of Original Greek Words*, Old Tappan, NJ: Fleming H. Revell, 1966.

---

[1] At the time that the different articles were written, the author made no attempt to be exhaustive in his reference to bibliography, nor has any attempt been made to update and supplement the references.

Webster's Seventh New Collegiate Dictionary, Springfield: G. & C. Merriam Company, 1966).